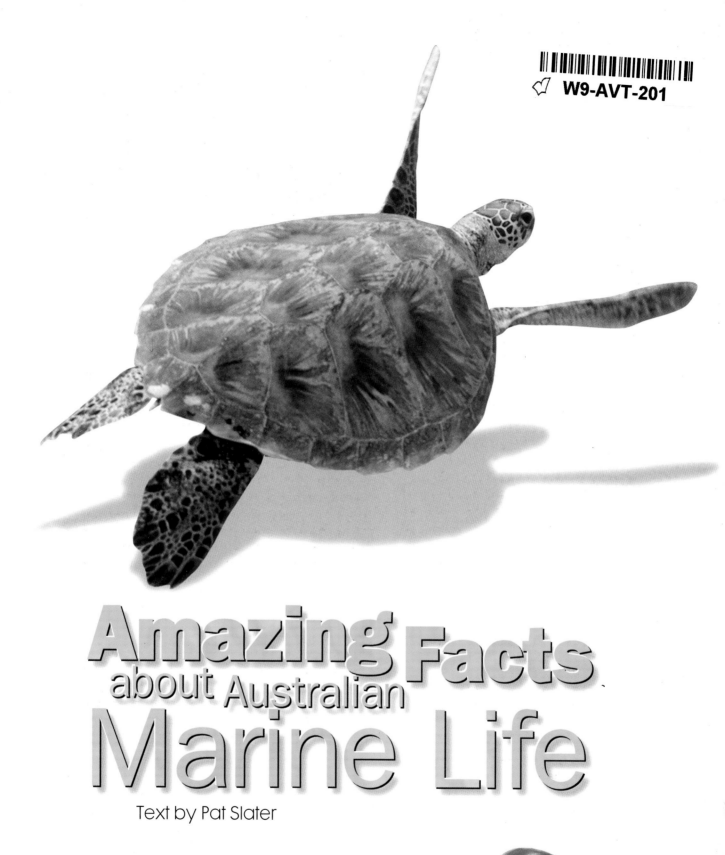

Amazing Facts
about Australian
Marine Life

Text by Pat Slater

Steve Parish
DISCOVER & LEARN
ABOUT AUSTRALIA

www.steveparish.com.au

Contents

Fascinating sea creatures

Discovering marine creatures

This Big-belly Seahorse is only one of the ocean's myriad of fascinating inhabitants

Distant ancestors of this Noble Feather Star existed in the oceans of 400 million years ago

Earth is the only planet in our solar system to have oceans. These oceans were the cradle of life on our world, and today they continue to make life on its surface possible.

Australia's coastline is over 36 000 kilometres in length – longer than the distance around the Earth. The majority of the population lives within a short distance of some part of this coastline. Many depend on the sea to provide a living, or go to it for recreation, relaxation or entertainment. A few people spend their lives investigating the ocean's physical features, or studying particular groups of its myriad of inhabitants.

Not everyone can be lucky enough to live by the sea or dive its depths. However, all of us can enjoy the fascination of sea creatures. This volume attempts to convey something of the diversity of the remarkable animals which live in our oceans.

The ocean is home to a diversity of life forms

Seals and sea-lions live most of their lives in the ocean, but come to land to breed

Crustaceans such as this Ghost Crab have colonised* the shore as well as the sea

Sea stars have adapted to many marine habitats, from shallows to ocean deeps

About this book

This book is intended to be an observer's introduction to some of the groups of marine creatures which may be observed in the seas and oceans around Australia.

The Index inside the back cover will give ready reference to the creatures pictured in the book. Look for words marked with an asterisk (*) in the Glossary on page 79. Places mentioned in the text are shown on the map on page 80, and some further reading is listed on the same page. Your local library will be able to help you with other reference works should you need more information.

In this book, the common name by which an animal is generally known is given capital letters, e.g., Humpback Whale. Where a group of animals is referred to, lower case initials are used, e.g., the baleen* whales. "Fish" is used to refer to one or more individuals of the same species*. "Fishes" refers to more than one species of fish.

Ocean creatures may live in associations which benefit both partners

A hatchling sea turtle, a marine reptile, skitters across the beach to its lifetime ocean home

Eels are fish and breathe oxygen from water

Life in the sea

Every part of the sea contains creatures of some sort, for it offers a variety of habitats*, from the area between tidelines to the deepest trenches.

Some animals drift or swim in the water, others fasten themselves to the sea floor, crawl across it, or burrow into it.

The nature of marine life and the forms it takes are influenced by the sunlight available, the temperature, pressure and movement of the water, and the nature of the sea floor beneath. Light can penetrate into clear sea water for about 200 metres, and it is in this lighted zone that plants grow and life is most abundant.

Waves are caused by wind blowing across the surface of the ocean

Sinking to the depths

For each 10 metres of descent into the ocean the pressure increases by one atmosphere (the pressure of air on the Earth's surface).

As depth increases, light fades and the water grows colder. In the deepest part of the ocean, the pressure is more than 1000 times that at the surface, it is always dark and the water temperature is just above freezing. No plants can grow there, for they need sunlight to make food, and animals of the depths eat each other, or eat food which sinks from the surface. Some deep sea animals produce their own, cold, light.

RAOUL SLATER

The intertidal zone is a harsh habitat for sea star, molluscs and barnacles

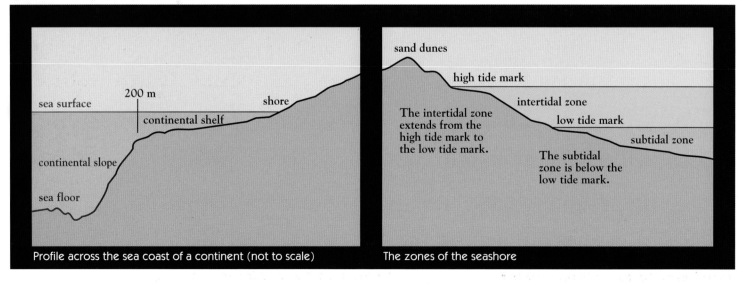

sea surface

200 m

shore

continental shelf

continental slope

sea floor

sand dunes

high tide mark

intertidal zone

The intertidal zone extends from the high tide mark to the low tide mark.

low tide mark

subtidal zone

The subtidal zone is below the low tide mark.

Profile across the sea coast of a continent (not to scale)

The zones of the seashore

Waves, tides and currents

A tide is a change in sea level caused by the pull of the Moon, or to a lesser extent the Sun, on the Earth. The pull causes the ocean to bulge, dragging it away from the land. Most places on Earth have two high tides and two low tides every 24 hours.

A **wave** is movement of surface water usually caused by wind. The wave form may travel, but the water itself does not flow far.

An **ocean current** is a moving mass of sea water driven by wind. Its direction is influenced by the rotation of the Earth on its axis. Currents swirl in great loops, clockwise to the north of the Equator, anti-clockwise to the south. They move at about the speed a human can walk and may carry warm or cold water. Some currents form "rivers in the sea".

Tidelines and mineral stains from freshwater springs mark this beach

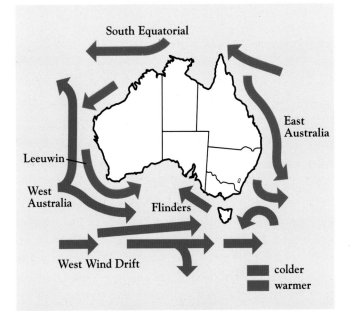

Major ocean currents occurring around the coast of Australia

Brittle stars can be found in the ocean depths

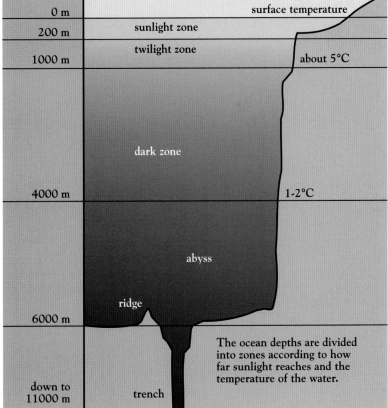

Depth	Zone	Temperature
0 m		surface temperature
200 m	sunlight zone	
1000 m	twilight zone	about 5°C
4000 m	dark zone	1-2°C
6000 m	abyss / ridge	
down to 11000 m	trench	

The ocean depths are divided into zones according to how far sunlight reaches and the temperature of the water.

Depth zones of the ocean (not drawn to scale)

7

How animals are named

Mouth of a Port Jackson Shark, *Heterodontus portusjacksoni*

Common names and scientific names

Taxonomists are people who describe, identify and name living organisms*. Worldwide, around two million land and marine animals and plants have been given scientific names by taxonomists so far.

Most creatures which appear in this book have been described by scientists and given scientific names. They may have a common name as well, but these names will vary from place to place, whereas scientific names will remain the same in all cultures and places.

So the creature whose many-toothed mouth is shown on the left may be known to shark-watchers as a "bullhead", an "oystercrusher" or a "tabbigaw". Its accepted common name is the Port Jackson Shark, and its scientific name is *Heterodontus portusjacksoni*.

Classifying animals into groups

A species is a group of similar animals which can breed with each other and produce fertile* offspring. The scientific name of a species consists of at least two words, always written in italics. The first word, the genus, which places the animal in a group of very similar animals, is written with a capital initial letter. The second word, the species, which belongs only to that particular animal, is always written with a lower case initial letter. If a second reference is made to the same genus, the genus is represented by its initial letter only, unless confusion might arise.

Taxonomists group animals with characteristics in common:

A **kingdom** is made up of phyla.
A **phylum** is made up of classes.
A **class** is made up of orders.
An **order** is made up of families.
A **family** is made up of genera.
A **genus** is made up of species.

Classification of Strawberry Cod

Kingdom: Animalia
Phylum: Chordata
Class: Actinopterygii
Order: Perciformes
Family: Serranidae
Genus: *Trachypoma*
Species: *T. macracanthus*

Some groups of marine creatures

GROUP OF ANIMALS	EXAMPLES IN THIS BOOK	CHARACTERISTICS	
MAMMALS	whales and dolphins dugongs seals and sea-lions	Vertebrate* animals which produce their own body heat, have hair growing from their skin, and produce milk to feed their young.	
BIRDS	penguins, tube-noses, pelicans, cormorants, gannets, frigatebirds, gulls and terns, oystercatchers, waders and others	Vertebrate animals which produce their own body heat, and have feathers and scales on their skin. Their bodies are adapted for flight.	
REPTILES	crocodiles marine turtles seasnakes	Vertebrate animals which do not produce their own body heat, have scales on their skin and breathe by taking oxygen from the air.	
FISHES	bony fishes cartilaginous fishes	Vertebrate animals which do not produce their own body heat, usually have scales, and breathe by taking oxygen from water through gills.	
ASCIDIANS	sea squirts	Marine animals which possess a notochord* in early free-swimming stage, then settle, become water-filtering invertebrates*.	
ECHINODERMS	feather stars, sea stars, brittle stars and basket stars sea urchins sea cucumbers	Headless invertebrates having five radial* divisions on the body. Skeleton consists of plates under skin. Movement is by tube feet.	
BRYOZOANS	moss animals (lace corals)	Colonial* invertebrates forming a lacework on solid surfaces. Feed through tentacles which contain extensions of the body cavity.	
MOLLUSCS	chitons bivalves gastropods, nudibranchs cephalopods	Have soft body, sometimes protected by shells, consisting of head, organ mass and gliding foot. All except bivalves, which lack head, have rasping tongue.	
CRUSTACEANS	barnacles shrimps, prawns, lobsters crabs	Joint-legged animals with outside skeleton, having body divided into working sections. Blood circulates in large spaces.	
WORMS	flatworms ribbon worms segmented worms	A flatworm has a mouth but no anus* and no large body cavity. A segmented worm has a digestive, nervous and circulatory system.	
COELENTERATES	comb jellies, hydroids sea jellies, hard corals, black corals, soft corals, fan corals sea anemones, tube anemones	Animals having stinging cells (nematocysts), body made up of two layers of cells, and a digestive cavity, called a coelenteron.	
SPONGES	sponges	Many-celled animals having no tissues or organs, mouth or nervous system. Feed by taking in water and filtering out nutrients*.	

FACTS

▶ The Mariana Trench, in the Pacific Ocean, is 11 038 m deep (Mt Everest is 8882 m high).

▶ There are more than 1360 billion cubic kilometres of water on Earth, most of it in the oceans and seas.

▶ When Earth's climate grows colder and some ocean water turns to ice, the level of the sea falls. For the past 6000 years, sea level has risen at the rate of 0.1 cm per year.

▶ Because of the substances dissolved in it, sea water must be colder than pure water to freeze (it does so at about -2°C).

▶ About one billion years ago, the oceans contained the same proportion of salt to water as they do today.

▶ The oldest known form of life on Earth, cyanobacteria, build spongy, sediment*-trapping mats which harden in layers to form stromatolites.

▶ Stromatolites can be found in sheltered water in Shark Bay, WA, the Persian Gulf, the Bahamas and Yellowstone Park, USA.

A timeline for marine life

PRESENT

QUATERNARY 2 million years ago	The rise of humans.
TERTIARY 65 million years ago	Mammals dominant.
CRETACEOUS 145 million years ago	Dinosaurs extinct. Most modern groups of bony fishes established. Bivalves become common.
JURASSIC 208 million years ago	Birds appear. True mammals appear.
TRIASSIC 245 million years ago	Marine reptiles include turtles, dolphin-like ichthyosaurs, lizard-like mosasaurs, long-necked plesiosaurs. Reef-building corals present in suitable seas.
PERMIAN 280 million years ago	Crocodiles. Reptiles diversify as amphibians decline. Loss of shallow seas leads to mass extinctions of trilobites* and some sorts of crinoids, ammonites and bryozoans.
CARBONIFEROUS 355 million years ago	First reptiles appear. Echinoderms, bryozoans dominant in sea. Algal-sponge reefs.
DEVONIAN 408 million years ago	Most jawless fishes extinct. Amphibians emerge on land. Lungfish breathe free air. Ammonites (molluscs with coiled shells).
SILURIAN 438 million years ago	Scorpion-like invertebrates invade land. Plants grow on land. Fishes with jaws and armour-like scales.
ORDOVICIAN 510 million years ago	Jawless fishes. First marine vertebrates. Corals, molluscs (including cephalopods, nautiloids). Stalked echinoderms (sea lilies). Bryozoans.
CAMBRIAN 540 million years ago	Complex marine invertebrates with hard exoskeletons* (e.g., echinoderms; joint-limbed, armoured trilobites.) Radiolarians, which still exist today. Early sponges.
550 million years ago 590 million years ago	Single-celled marine animals with hard skeletons. Soft-bodied, many-celled animals such as worms, sea jellies and sea anemones exist in the sea, perhaps as early as 680 million year ago.
PRECAMBRIAN 2100 million years ago 3500 million years ago	

Cyanobacteria like those that formed these stromatolites existed 3500 million years ago

JIRI LOCHMAN

Some of Australia's coastal habitats

Tidal waterfalls

Wave-eroded sandstone

Continental island

Human-made habitat

Tidal mudflats with mangroves

Estuaries and coastal fringing mangroves

Sandy sea floor

Limestone, tilted, exposed and eroded

Coral cay, reef flat and lagoon

Sand island with stabilising vegetation

Sandstone cliffs

Rock platforms and fringing reefs

Sheltered bay and ocean beach

Giants feeding on pygmies

In the sunlit surface layers of the ocean live huge numbers of tiny plants. These are known as the phytoplankton. Feeding on these, and on each other, are tiny animals, the zooplankton. They form the basis of many food chains.

Planktonic larva* of a barnacle

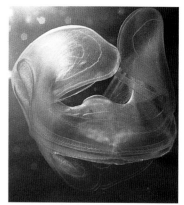

Planktonic comb jelly

GEOFF TAYLOR

Whale Shark

Straining for food

The Whale Shark, the largest living fish, may reach 12 metres in length. It feeds on tiny planktonic creatures, hanging in the water, opening its vast mouth and allowing water to rush in. Screens formed from its gill slits filter out food organisms.

Flying saucer

The disc-bodied Manta Ray may measure nearly 7 metres across its "wings". It has no teeth in its upper jaw and feeds on plankton sieved from the water through gills adapted as filtering plates. This enormous, harmless "devilray" may leap clear of the water, landing with a thunderous impact.

The huge Manta Ray feeds on tiny plankton

Tiny-throated giants

Humpback Whales belong to a group known as the baleen whales, which includes the Blue Whale, the largest animal ever to have lived on Earth. Baleen plates fringed with bristles hanging from the roofs of their mouths filter tiny creatures, especially the shrimp-like krill, from sea water.

MARK SIMMONS

A Humpback Whale eats shrimp-like krill

The sea anemone catches small creatures. Its commensal* crab feeds on plankton and debris

The sea urchin, with five jaws in a mouth on its underside, grazes on algae and encrusting animals

The Loggerhead Turtle crunches up molluscs, sea urchins, crabs and sea jellies with its horny jaws

The Australian Sea-lion catches fish, and squid beaks have been found in the stomachs of dead animals

The Thicklip Wrasse grubs in the sea floor for worms, molluscs and other small invertebrates

Sponges draw in water, filter out any plant or animal material it contains, then pass it out again

Shore birds probe mud or sand with their long bills and pull out any small animals they find

A Lionfish will stalk crabs and shrimps, its movement camouflaged* by its spines and stripes

HOW SOME ANIMALS OBTAIN FOOD FROM THE OCEAN

FACTS

▶ The "food chains" of the ocean begin with plants, which make food from nutrients in water and sunlight. They are eaten by herbivores* and omnivores*. In turn, these animals are eaten by carnivores* or, when they die, by scavengers*.

▶ In some sunless, deep parts of the ocean floor there are vents through which hot, mineral-rich water gushes out. Using sulphur in the water, bacteria* make food which supports clams, tube worms, shrimps and other animals.

▶ Not all large sea creatures eat small prey. A Sperm Whale, which can weigh up to 70 tonnes, may eat about 4% of its body weight in squid each day. One Giant Squid found in a Sperm Whale's stomach weighed 200 kg.

▶ The saying "eat or be eaten" can well be applied to fishes. Many fish have expandable jaws and elastic stomachs which allow them to swallow prey only marginally smaller than they are themselves.

▶ A commensal is a creature which benefits from living with another, which is neither helped nor harmed.

Powered by sunlight

Red alga often grows at deeper sunlit levels

Turtle weed, a hair-like green alga

Without marine plants, marine animals could not exist. There are two kinds of marine plants. Algae, or seaweeds, are simple in structure though, like more complicated plants, they can use energy from sunlight to make food. Seagrasses, relatives of flowering land plants, have leaves, stems and roots, and produce flowers and seeds.

Green alga grows in shallower water

The world's largest alga

The giant kelps are brown algae whose fronds are made buoyant by bladders. The tip of a giant kelp frond may be 45 metres from the holdfast which attaches the plant to the ocean floor. A forest of giant kelp provides habitats for a variety of animals, many found nowhere else.

Algae on a rock platform must withstand wave action

AN UNDERSEA GIANT

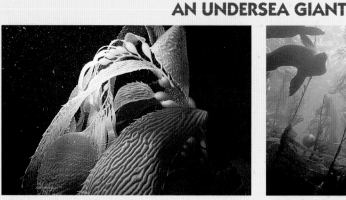
Bladders help a giant kelp frond remain buoyant

Australian Fur-seals playing amongst giant kelp

A seahorse swimming across a seagrass meadow. Seahorses eat tiny shrimps, not plants

Seagrass surrounds an Edmond's Sea Star

Pastures of the ocean

Australia has over 30 species of seagrasses, which are related to flowering plants. They are nurseries for fishes and prime feeding grounds for turtles, dugongs and many invertebrates. A seagrass meadow provides nutritious grazing, because bacteria, algae and single-celled plants live on the seagrass leaves and add to their food value.

KNEE-DEEP IN THE SEA

A mangrove tree puts out prop roots and aerial roots

These fruits and root-stems will drop into the ocean, drift and finally plant themselves in a suitable situation

Mangrove trees grow on the frontier between land and sea, stabilising shorelines and providing habitat for all sorts of marine creatures. The salt in the sea water drawn in by their roots is "sweated" out of the leaves, or is stored in mature leaves, which are then shed. Prop roots hold a mangrove tree on sand or mud, and trap debris to nourish it. Aerial roots take in oxygen when high tide submerges the lower parts of the tree.

Living filters

A sponge consists of layers of cells surrounding cavities lined by special cells called collar cells. Each collar cell protrudes a whip-like process into the cavity. The waving action of these draws water into the sponge through tiny holes or pores called ostia. The collar cells take food particles from the water, which is then pumped out of large, volcano-like vents called oscules.

Sponges may be brightly coloured

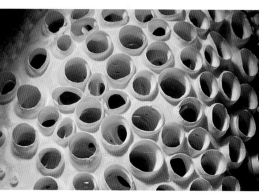
Oscules, the openings through which water exits

A body in the bath

Sponges have soft tissues, but are firm to touch. They are supported by skeletons made of hard spicules* of limestone or glassy silica, or a meshwork of soft, silky fibres called spongin. Some have both spicules and spongin. Once, people used sponge skeletons to scrub their bodies.

A sponge is shaped by the conditions of its habitat

"Finger" formation maximises water entry area

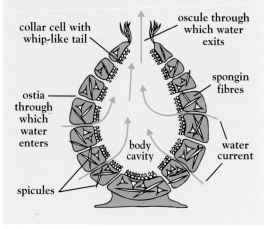
Body plan of a sponge (cut down the middle)

collar cell with whip-like tail
oscule through which water exits
spongin fibres
ostia through which water enters
body cavity
water current
spicules

The Holey Sponge may grow to 45 cm in height

FACTS

▶ Worldwide, about 10 000 species of sponge have been named by scientists.

▶ Sponges first appeared in the Cambrian period, 570–500 million years ago. They have not changed much in the 450 million years since Devonian times, when they were the major form of life in shallow seas.

▶ Until the early 19th century, sponges were thought to be plants. They are now placed in Phylum *Porifera* (meaning pored, or holed, animals).

▶ The smallest sponges are microscopic. The largest, found in the Antarctic, are 2 m across.

An Orange Sponge

▶ Sponges produce eggs which, when fertilised, become tiny drifting larvae. When they reach a suitable place, these larvae settle and change into adult sponges.

Water purifiers

Sponges are filter-feeders, which take in water then strain off tiny plants and animals, bacteria and oxygen before pumping it out again. These living sieves are abundant in areas exposed to strong currents, where vigorously circulating water brings them plenty of food. A typical sponge pumps through 4 to 5 times its own volume of water each day. A football-sized sponge will filter several thousand litres of water each day.

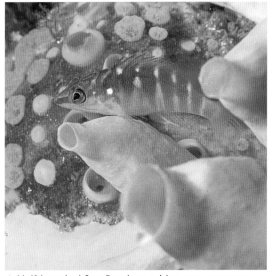
A Half-banded Sea Perch perching on a sponge

The purple material is an encrusting sponge. Sponges often form thin crusts on solid objects

This sponge is used by feather stars to reach plankton-rich currents. The fish is a Red Rockcod

Three species of sponge sharing a habitat

Three sponge species

Hollow-bodied stingers

Coelenterates have bodies consisting of an inner and an outer layer of cells, separated by a jelly-like substance. These layers enclose a body cavity: the coelenteron. The mouth is the only opening into or out of the body, and food is digested in the body cavity. The outer layer includes cells called nematocysts, which dart out threads which poison or entangle prey. Stinging coelenterates include sea jellies, sea anemones and corals.

The life history of a stinging coelenterate may include a free-swimming larva, a bell-shaped, drifting medusa* and a fixed, solitary* or colonial* polyp*.

Sea drifters

Sea jellies are usually found in numbers in shallow water. Their fragile, jelly-like bodies break down quickly when washed up on shore.

A sea jelly's mouth is on its

This large sea jelly is found in estuaries and tidal rivers

underside, in the middle of hanging folds, or tentacles, which carry stinging cells. Around the edge of the jelly's "bell" are many marginal tentacles and sense organs. A sea jelly is either male or female, and the reproductive organs can be seen through the bell.

The white areas are reproductive organs

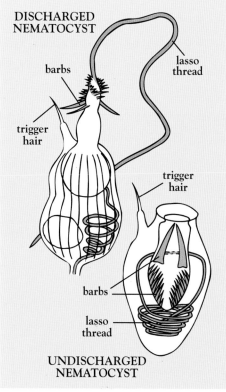

Undischarged and discharged nematocysts

DISCHARGED NEMATOCYST

barbs

lasso thread

trigger hair

trigger hair

barbs

lasso thread

UNDISCHARGED NEMATOCYST

Tiny fish fry* may live under the shelter of a sea jelly's bell

LIFE HISTORY OF THE MOON SEA JELLY

Adult sea jelly medusa is male or female. Sperm enter female through mouth.

Ephyrae break free and develop into sea jelly medusae.

Fertilised egg is shed and develops into larva, which drifts with plankton.

Larva settles on a firm surface where current brings food.

Polyp divides into eight-armed buds called ephyrae.

Larva grows into an eight-armed polyp.

Stinging hydrozoan can deliver a painful "bite"

Hydrozoan polyps eat floating plankton

Fire on the reef

Hydrozoans are related to sea jellies. Groups of tiny polyps carry out different functions: some are specialised* for feeding, some carry out reproduction, and some defend the colony* by delivering powerful stings which have earned one hydrozoan group the name fire corals.

A solitary hydroid spreads its tentacles to catch food

Fire coral carries powerful stinging cells

FACTS

▶ Hydrozoans may be solitary, but usually form colonies, with individuals connected by extensions of the body cavity.

▶ The Bluebottle is a hydrozoan colony which drifts on the ocean under a float. Trailing tentacles, sometimes 10 m long, kill small animals, which are then pulled in to the mouths of the feeding polyps. Some fish shelter between the tentacles.

float

individual polyps hang under float

short feeding tentacles

long tentacles with stinging cells

BLUEBOTTLE

19

FACTS

▶ Sea anemones have special "fighting" tentacles, used to combat nearby anemones.

SEA ANEMONES

Deadly beauty

A sea anemone is a large polyp whose feeding tentacles are held aloft on a cylindrical body called the column. The tentacles surround the mouth and each one contains hundreds of stinging cells. These are used to capture the plankton and small creatures on which the anemone feeds.

An anemone's tentacles look like fleshy flower petals

Closeup of the tentacles of an anemone

Supplementary feeding

The tentacles of many anemones contain algae known as zooxanthellae.

These algae use sunlight, carbon dioxide and water to produce substances which provide the host anemones with an important element of their food intake. Because of the association, most big anemones are found in shallow, sunlit water. The algae give the anemone's tentacles a brownish or greenish tinge.

▶ Most anemones seem fixed in place, though some use the basal disc to creep about, while a few drift.

▶ Anemones can grow from pieces of an adult, or a fertilised egg hatches into a drifting larva, which eventually settles and changes to an adult.

Tube anemones have double rows of tentacles

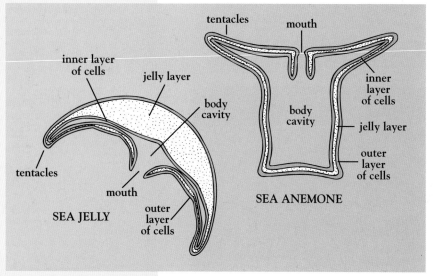

A sea jelly medusa and an adult sea anemone have similar body plans

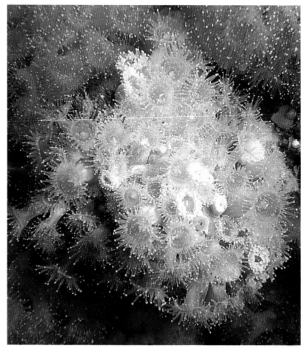

Colonial anemones spread their tentacles in the current

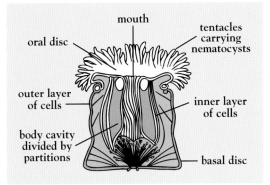

Body plan of a sea anemone

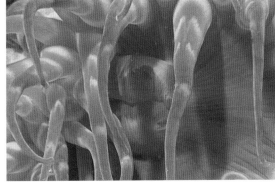

Tentacles, oral disc and mouth of a sea anemone

Turning an enemy into an ally

The stinging cells of anemones kill small fish on contact, and then convey the prey to their mouths. However, anemonefish, also called clownfish, live in anemones and so gain protection from predators*. An anemonefish presents its pelvic fins and tail to an anemone's tentacles, makes light contact, retreats, then repeats the process. Gradually fish and anemone become desensitised* to each other and finally the fish remains unharmed. A group of anemonefish will take an anemone as their territory* and chase other fish away from it.

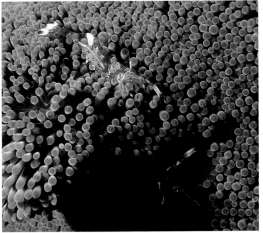

Shrimps may make their homes in anemones

The Orange-fin Anemonefish grows to 14 cm in length

A Pink Anemonefish nestles in the shelter of its host sea anemone. It is found around the northern coast

DID YOU KNOW?

FACTS

▶ Coral reefs are found where the temperature of the sea water ranges from 18–33°C.

▶ About 500 species of hard corals are known from the Indo-Pacific area. About 70% of these are found on reefs off Australia.

▶ Coral polyps which live in colonies are linked by tissue. All share food which becomes available in any section of the colony.

▶ Coral reefs have been present on Earth for over 240 million years.

▶ Every square metre of an active coral reef manufactures between 10 and 30 grams of limestone from sea water each day.

▶ A coral polyp "house" has a floor, outer walls and a number of internal partitions. New polyps build their houses on top of dead ones, laying down new floors over old roofs.

A solitary coral polyp

The corals which contain zooxanthellae grow where sunlight can reach their food-making inhabitants

A blenny makes its home in a coral cavity

Homes of stone

Coral reefs are made up of limestone cases, each surrounding the body of an anemone-like coral polyp. Each polyp builds its case from calcium it takes from sea water.

Reef-building corals are known as hard, or true, corals. Each polyp has six, or multiples of six, tentacles around its mouth. Most corals extend their tentacles to feed at night, when reef zooplankton is most active.

DAYTIME BEAUTY

Sunshine coral is unusual because its polyps (seen above left in closeup) feed during daytime

Staghorn corals branch most strongly in calmer, deeper water

Low-profile corals can withstand wave action

Partners

The fastest-growing corals have algae called zooxanthellae living in the tissues of the polyps. The algae use sunlight and the waste products of the polyp to make oxygen and food substances, which leak into the surrounding tissues of the polyp and can

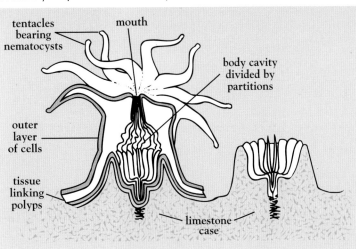

Body plan of a coral polyp, and (right) the case left when the animal dies

provide up to 98% of its food needs. Corals containing zooxanthellae are found in shallow, clear, sunlit water. Corals found in deeper water, in places too dark for zooxanthellae to flourish, are slower-growing. Zooxanthellae are yellow-brown in colour and corals containing them are usually fawn, brown or green.

ZOANTHIDS: relatives of sea anemones and corals

A zoanthid polyp looks like a small anemone, but has no basal disc. It has one or two rings of smooth, slender tentacles and is connected to other zoanthid polyps at the base.

FACTS

▶ The shape of a coral colony depends on its environment. A species which grows in a rounded mass in areas with strong wave action may produce slender branches in deeper, calmer water.

▶ Because one species of hard coral may vary in formation and colour, it is easiest to identify corals from details of their skeletons after they are dead.

▶ A coral polyp's body cavity, like that of a sea anemone, is divided by partitions which increase the area for digesting food.

▶ The relationship of mutual benefit between coral polyp and zooxanthellae is known as symbiosis.

▶ The limestone skeleton which encases the coral polyps is white, and the brightly coloured dead coral sold to tourists has been artificially coloured.

▶ A zoanthid is a coral relative which does not have a skeleton. Zoanthids may fasten themselves to the surfaces of sponges or other corals.

▶ Fertiliser and sewage runoff from the land may encourage growth of algae on a reef. Larval Crown-of-thorns graze this algae and later become coral-eating adults.

▶ The Crown-of-thorns may return in plague numbers every 17 years.

A mushroom coral is a solitary polyp which lies free on the ocean floor

▶ Scientists studying a 7 ha reef discovered that the corals added 206 tonnes of limestone each year, but that 123 tonnes of reef were lost to boring sponges, grazing fishes, sea urchins and other creatures. (The Crown-of-thorns was not involved in this study.)

▶ Coral which is stressed by rising water temperature or pollution may expel its zooxanthellae, bleaching out and eventually dying.

Coral-consumers

Coral colonies are attacked by a number of predators. Parrotfishes chew up coral skeletons and digest polyps and algae, and other sorts of fishes nip off the polyps. Worms and molluscs burrow into the coral, and molluscs called drupes are coral-eating specialists.

The Crown-of-thorns Sea Star, which eats coral polyps, may reach plague numbers on some reefs. This giant sea star may be 70 cm across, and its spines, which can be 5 cm in length, are tipped with toxin*. In the mid 1980s, Crown-of-thorns destroyed about 150 coral reefs on the Great Barrier Reef.

One of the few predators on adult Crown-of-thorns is the Triton Conch, which has been over-harvested by shell collectors in many reef areas.

Leaf coral grows in plates

Vase coral may grow to one metre across

Plate coral provides many refuges for fish and other reef inhabitants

JUST A FEW NIGHTS EACH YEAR

Coral polyps may divide to form new individuals (staghorn coral may add 50 cm per year to the tips of its "antlers" by division). Corals also reproduce sexually*. A polyp may be both male and female, or only male, or only female. Mass spawning, or release of eggs and sperm, takes place on the Great Barrier Reef one or two nights after the full moon in November. For several nights, millions of eggs and sperm are released from coral polyps and float to the surface. Those fertilised eggs which escape predators hatch into larvae and drift with the plankton. Finally, a tiny percentage of the larvae manage to settle on the reef and begin new coral colonies.

ROB ADLAND

Coral polyps spawn on a few nights each year

Butterflyfish are brilliantly coloured tropical reef fish with very pointed snouts and brush-like, recurving (backwards bending) teeth. Some of this group feed on coral polyps. The Long-nose Butterflyfish has a particularly elongated, forceps-like snout, which is useful for probing crevices in coral and retrieving tiny creatures to eat. The Long-nose above is cruising over a brain coral. A single brain coral polyp 1 mm in diameter can, by dividing, form a colony over 3 m high. Such a colony may be nearly 1000 years old.

FACTS
ABOUT AUSTRALIA'S GREAT BARRIER REEF

▶ The Great Barrier Reef stretches for 2000 km along the Qld coast. It covers 344 000 km² of the Pacific Ocean.

▶ The Reef is made up of over 2500 individual coral reefs, containing around 400 species of coral. It includes about 70 named coral cays, as well as many other islands.

▶ More than 2000 species of fish live in Reef waters.

▶ Aboriginal people could walk to the outer Barrier Reef 18 000 years ago. By 12 000 years ago, rising sea levels had flooded the coastal plain and the process of coral reef-building had begun.

▶ The Great Barrier Reef Marine Park Authority was established in 1975, and the Reef was proclaimed a World Heritage Area in October 1981.

▶ The Great Barrier Reef can be seen from a space shuttle circling Earth.

FACTS

▶ Soft corals occur in numbers at depths between 10 and 30 m. They remind some divers of fields of undersea wildflowers.

▶ Some soft corals may wander slowly around the reef, extending the tissues in their bases in the direction of travel.

▶ Gorgonians flourish on the reef's steep outer slopes. A gorgonian may grow to 3 m across, at an angle which gives it the best exposure to food-carrying currents.

Soft coral polyps

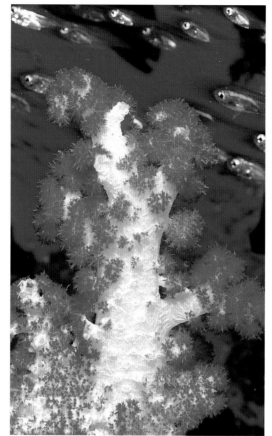

Soft coral is protected by fine spicules

Soft corals

A soft coral polyp has eight feathery tentacles and eight internal partitions. Its tissues are supported by tiny internal spicules of calcium, called sclerites.

Most soft corals are colonial and polyps can reproduce themselves by budding off new individuals. Many contain zooxanthellae. The brilliant colours of some species are due to pigments* contained in their sclerites.

Each gorgonian polyp has eight plumed tentacles

Living lace

Gorgonian corals, which include sea fans and sea whips, are eight-tentacled corals with horny external skeletons of gorgonin. They are often brightly coloured.

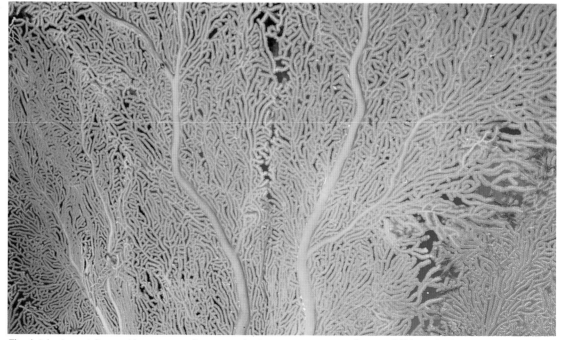

The intricate net formed by a gorgonian spreads across a current and traps drifting plankton

The polyps of black coral range from white to brown

A hawkfish takes refuge on a stem of black coral

Black at the heart

Black corals have six-tentacled, brown, yellow or white polyps, which cannot draw back into their bases. The horn-like inner skeleton supporting a colony is black. The skeletons of varieties of black coral, particularly those found at depths below 50 metres, may be cut and polished to make jewellery.

Writing on water

A sea pen consists of a colony of polyps growing on branches which spread on either side of a central stalk, like barbs on an ostrich feather. Sea pens grow on mud or sand on the sea floor, often in large groups. They usually spend the day withdrawn into the mud or sand, and expand into the water to catch plankton at night.

A sea pen being eaten by two nudibranchs

A sea pen expanded to catch plankton at night

FACTS

▶ Soft corals avoid being overgrown by algae or sponges by producing special chemicals. Medical researchers are investigating these as possible anti-cancer drugs for human use.

▶ Some sea pens may produce a ghostly blue, green or violet light when disturbed. The largest sea pens reach a height of 1 m.

▶ The stem of a sea whip may be home to a pair of gobies, each tiny fish only 2–3 cm long.

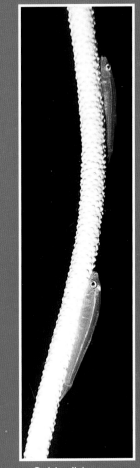
Gobies living on a sea whip stem

Slitherers, creepers

Dramatic coloration may signal a flatworm tastes bad or is toxic*

The general name "worms" is applied to many sorts of legless, burrowing, gliding or creeping creatures. Some are free-living, others are parasites*. There are many unrelated major groups of worms living in the ocean and shore.

▶ A study made at Heron Island, at the southern end of the Great Barrier Reef, showed that 1400 worms belonging to 103 species lived in a single small coral head.

▶ If a flatworm is cut into several pieces, some pieces may grow into new individuals.

▶ Marine flatworms are both male and female (hermaphrodite*). A pair may exchange sperm and reproduce sexually.

▶ Most flatworms are predators, crawling over and engulfing their prey with their muscular pharynx.

▶ Some flatworms live on the outside of other creatures, such as crays, feeding on small organisms in the surrounding water.

A flatworm appears to glide over a reef

A flatworm has no external gills

Flat-bodied gliders

Free-living marine flatworms have oval, flattened bodies, covered with minute bristles. They glide slowly, sliding across a mat of mucus they have laid down, powered by the movement of the bristles on their undersides. A flatworm can push out the muscular first part of its digestive canal, the pharynx*, to seize food.

mouth (under body)

pharynx pokes out of mouth

eyespot

branched digestive canal

brain

Body plan of a free-living flatworm

Lengthy predators

Ribbon worms are long, flat-bodied and unsegmented. They feed on invertebrates or their eggs, grasping them with a proboscis* extending from the front of the head. Many produce protective chemicals, some of which are being investigated for medical use. Some ribbon worms can endure high levels of heavy metals in their habitat and survive where the sea has been polluted by industrial wastes.

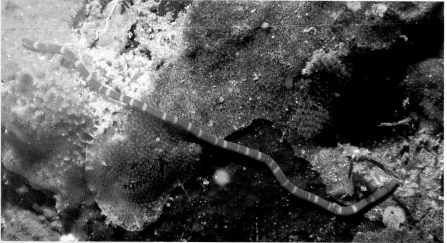

A ribbon worm's body is not divided into segments

A bristle worm displays the paddle-like, bristled flaps on its sides

proboscis pushed out of the mouth
jaws
eye
tentacle
flap bearing bristles
body segment

Plan of bristle worm forebody

Some have bristle-feet, some have feather-heads

Marine segmented worms belong to the same phylum as the garden earthworm.

Bristle-footed marine worms have a fleshy, paddle-like flap, set with bundles of bristles, projecting from the side of each segment. The first body segment bears sense organs, the second bears the mouth, which has hard, pincer-like jaws set on a muscular pharynx. The giant worms which are found buried in sand at low-water mark from Queensland to South Australia belong to this group.

Tube-worms build their homes of mud, sand or limestone. Their bodies are streamlined and their head appendages* have been replaced by branched crowns, which filter food and oxygen from the water.

A feather duster worm

A Christmas Tree Worm extends its feeding crown

A feather duster worm surrounded by coral polyps

29

In full armour

Female crab guarding eggs

Crustaceans belong to the group called arthropods, or joint-legged animals, which includes insects, spiders and scorpions.

Like other arthropods, the crustaceans wear rigid external skeletons, which must be moulted* at intervals as the animal's body grows. Usually a crustacean's body can be divided into cephalothorax (head plus thorax) and abdomen. The front part of the body may be hidden by a plate called the carapace*. Crustaceans have jointed limbs, which can move in all directions and are used for many purposes. Unlike other arthropods, crustaceans have two pairs of antennae*. Crabs, crays and shrimps belong to a group of ten-legged crustaceans called decapods, whose carapace stretches down on either side of the body and encloses the gills.

Soldier crabs march across the intertidal area. Unlike most crabs, they can move forwards

Move like a crab

A true crab has no obvious tail, and the abdomen may be bent forward so it is protected by the carapace. The body cannot be flexed or twisted, and to make up for this the eyes are perched on movable stalks. Most crabs scuttle sideways, the legs on one side of the body pushing, while the legs on the other side pull.

IAN MORRIS

A male fiddler crab waves a large nipper in a threat display

This horned pebble crab buries itself in sand

The Mud Crab lives in a burrow among mangrove roots. It is a popular human food

IAN MORRIS

This crab takes refuge in sea anemone tentacles

A crab which lives amongst a sea star's tube feet

FACTS

▶ The gills of crustaceans lie in spaces under the carapace. A pair of beating appendages keeps water flowing over the gills.

▶ Some crabs can spend long periods out of water. Their gills are kept moist in their gill chambers and are stiffened and spaced to obtain the most possible oxygen from the air.

▶ Some hermit crabs roam the beach hunting for food, and the shell gathered by a human beachcomber may suddenly grow legs and scramble hastily away.

▶ A common family of hermit crabs is called *Diogenidae*, after the ancient Greek philosopher Diogenes who lived in a barrel.

A crab which camouflages its carapace with other animals

Seeking protection

Crabs form prey for a variety of marine and seashore creatures and adopt various ways of protecting themselves.

Some crabs live in the shelter of anemone tentacles, or amongst the tube feet of sea stars. Some are hidden by sponges or sea anemones on their carapace. Boxer crabs wear an anemone on each nipper.

Hermit crabs have long, soft abdomens, which they protect by occupying the discarded shells of gastropods (see p. 36). When slipping from a smaller to a larger shell they are vulnerable to predators, but this is also the only time that they can mate.

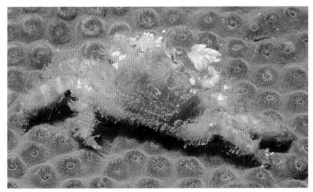
This boxer crab wears a sea anemone on each claw

A hermit crab protects its soft abdomen in a mollusc shell

A hermit crab keeps keen watch from its entrance

FACTS

▶ Australia's rock lobsters are sometimes called crays, but that name is more often applied to freshwater species. The European Lobster has great claws on its first pair of legs.

▶ Three species of rock lobster are caught commercially around Australian coasts.

▶ The most valuable Australian fisheries are based on prawns. The major prawn fishery extends from Koolan Island, WA, to Cape York, Qld.

▶ A female lobster carrying eggs is said to be "in berry".

▶ Slipper lobsters, such as the Moreton Bay Bug and Balmain Bug, have wide carapaces and broad, flattened antennae.

▶ Research on the compound* eye of the mantis shrimp carried out at the University of Queensland may prove useful for the robotics industry. The shrimp's eye has 16 types of vision receptors, including 12 for colour analysis. They lie on a central band, which moves constantly to scan the surroundings.

The Painted Rock Lobster may grow to 46 cm. This one has its muscular tail tucked under its body

Tails they lose!

The cephalothorax of a lobster, prawn or shrimp consists of 13 or 14 fused segments, covered by a carapace. The head carries two longer antennae and two shorter antennules.

The abdomen consists of flexible segments and ends in a tail fan. Unfortunately for these creatures, the muscles which power their abdomens are considered tasty by humans.

A slipper lobster has broad, flattened antennae

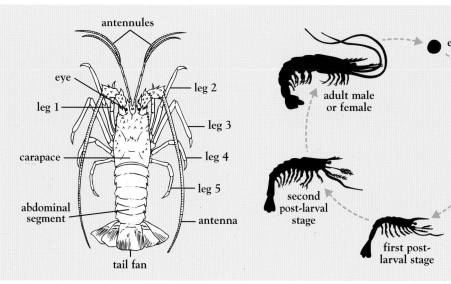

An adult rock lobster (left) and the life history of a prawn. Most crustaceans have one or more larval stages

This shrimp makes its home under a rock

The Banded Coral Shrimp cleans fishes

Clawed cleaners

Most crustaceans spend daylight hiding, but a group of shrimps are day shift workers. Cleaner shrimps wait at "stations" for fish to arrive and signal by the way they hang in the water that they wish to be cleaned. The shrimps crawl over them, even into mouths and under gill covers, removing and eating small parasites. They also nibble the mucus coating the fish.

Hingebeak shrimps

BARNACLES – HITCH-HIKERS OF THE SEAS

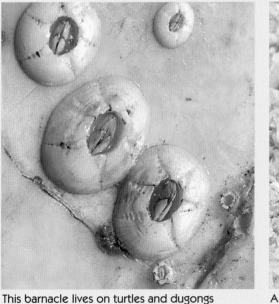
This barnacle lives on turtles and dugongs

A barnacle which lives on molluscs and crabs

Barnacles have free-swimming larvae which use a glue-like substance to attach themselves head-down to chosen surfaces. They then grow shells made up of plates, and extend jointed appendages through the openings to feed on plankton.

DID YOU KNOW?

FACTS

▶ Worldwide, there are about 100 000 species of molluscs. Most species (around 75 000) are gastropods (see p. 36). The most visible molluscs, the cephalopods (see p. 42), which include the octopuses and squids, number only about 650 species.

▶ Bivalves account for 15 000 to 20 000 species, and include clams, cockles, mussels, oysters and shipworms.

All foot and stomach

Molluscs have soft bodies, divided into a head (not present in bivalves), a muscular foot and a hump containing the body organs. A fold of skin, the mantle, forms a pocket which may contain gills, anus and reproductive opening.

The blue spots on the mantle of this scallop are eyes

Bivalve molluscs

The body of a bivalve mollusc is flattened from side to side and is attached to both its shells. The shell is hinged and held together by teeth and sockets on the hinge line. The animal has no head and its two mantle lobes may form two tubes, one to take in sea water, the other to pass it out again. Using these siphons, a buried bivalve can still eat and breathe.

Camouflaged by sand, a scallop opens to feed

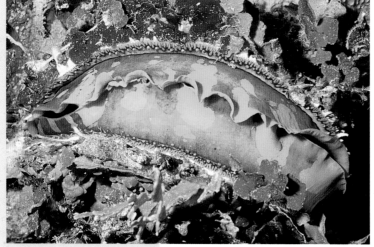

A gaping thorny oyster shows a brilliantly coloured mantle

Once the oyster closes, encrusting growths will camouflage its shell

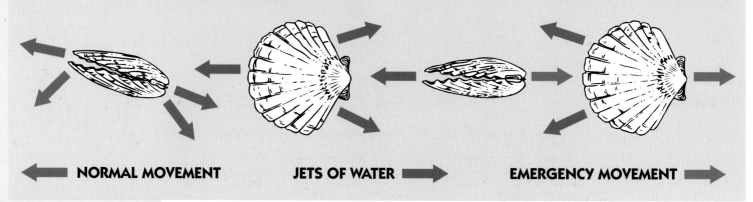

NORMAL MOVEMENT   **JETS OF WATER**   **EMERGENCY MOVEMENT**

The mantle lobes of a scallop are not attached to the shell margins. If threatened, a scallop claps its shell and shoots backwards

The giant clam's mantle lobes are fused together. A jet of water can be forced out of the siphon in the centre

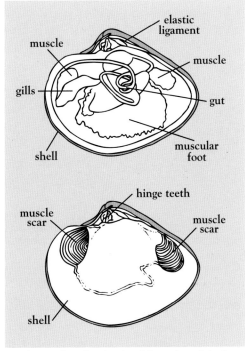

Bivalve mollusc body plan (above) and shell

The greatest clam

The largest and heaviest of all bivalves is the Giant Clam. One pair of shells, collected from the Great Barrier Reef in 1917, weighs 263.4 kilograms and measures 1.09 x 0.75 metres. When alive, the animal inside weighed around 10 kilograms.

Due to over-harvesting for human food, giant clams are almost extinct in some areas of the Pacific.

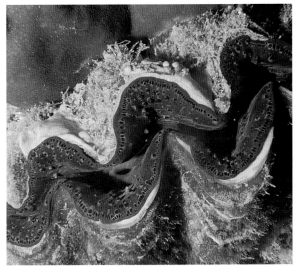

Giant clam shows eyespots along its mantle

How a pearl is formed

A commercial pearl is formed when a grain of sand or some other substance lodges between a pearl oyster's mantle and its shell. The mantle produces layers of calcium carbonate, like those lining the shell, to cover the irritating object and to prevent it harming the oyster's soft body. Today, most pearls are cultured in farms.

The largest round pearl recorded, *La Peregrina* (the Wanderer), was found in the Gulf of Panama, given by Philip II of Spain to England's Mary Tudor, and eventually presented to film star Elizabeth Taylor.

FACTS

▶ Scallops, mussels, clams and oysters are among the few marine foods to be farmed rather than gathered.

▶ The Goolwa Cockle, or pipi, lives just under the surface of sand and is widely used for bait.

▶ The teredo, or shipworm, burrows into wood with its paired shells. It causes great damage to jetties and wooden vessels.

▶ A Giant Clam shuts too slowly and jerkily to trap a human foot.

▶ Clams harbour food-producing zooxanthellae in the tissues of their brightly-coloured mantles.

EIGHT PLATES AND A GIRDLE

Chitons live on rocky ocean shores, their soft parts protected by shells consisting of eight plates embedded in a fleshy, sometimes spiny, girdle. They creep around at night on a fleshy foot and when the tide is out hide from the sunlight in shady hollows. Even the shell plates seem to be sensitive to light.

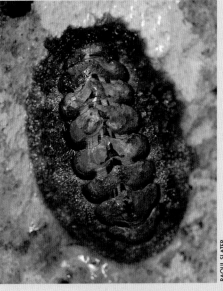

RAOUL SLATER

A gastropod mollusc on the move, heading to the left

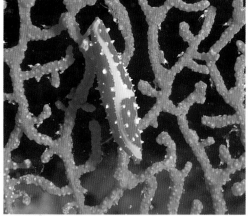
This spindle cowrie is found only on gorgonians

This egg cowrie eats soft corals

DID YOU KNOW?

FACTS

▶ Gastropod molluscs have a radula, a tongue like a ribbon covered with horny teeth, used for capturing prey and rasping off food particles.

▶ A cowrie shell's long opening is shaped to allow water to flow efficiently through the gill chamber.

▶ The shell of a cowrie is polished each time the mantle slides over it. A cowrie stops growing once it reaches sexual maturity. The lip of its shell curls inwards and the shell grows thicker, but no longer.

▶ Trochus shell was once cut into "mother-of-pearl" buttons – now superseded by plastic.

▶ A stromb uses its sharp-edged operculum as a weapon of defence, or to right itself when turned on its back.

Stomach-footed animals

At the front of a gastropod mollusc is a head bearing a mouth, eyes and tentacles. Behind the head is a muscular foot, on top of which is a hump containing the internal organs.

The hump is draped with skin-like membrane, the mantle, which produces the shell. The mantle encloses a cavity which hides the gills, mucus glands, openings for the reproductive system, the anus, through which pass wastes from the gut, and organs which are sensitive to chemicals in the water. In most gastropods this hump is coiled, and in many it has twisted around so that the mantle cavity lies above the head. This process is called torsion. Water is drawn into the mantle cavity through a fold of the mantle edge called the anterior siphon and passes out again through the posterior siphon. These siphons may be supported by folds of the outer lip of the shell. Usually a gastropod can withdraw head and foot into its shell, often sealing the entrance with an operculum* on its foot.

A cowrie covered by its brilliant mantle

The operculum is a "door" attached to the mollusc's foot

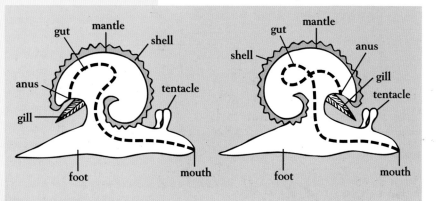
Plan of the gastropod body before torsion (left) and after torsion (right)

gut | mantle | shell | anus | tentacle | gill | foot | mouth

36

Meat and veg

Abalones, limpets, trochus and turban shells are vegetarians, which use the radula to rasp algae. Many other gastropods are carnivores: the radula is adapted to drill holes in the shells of prey, or to bite. A carnivore's shell can be identified by the canal, or groove, at the front of its opening. A vegetarian's shell has no such groove.

Holes around an abalone shell channel water out

The Banded Helmet Shell eats sand-dwellers

A gastropod engulfing a bivalve mollusc with its foot

VENOMOUS BARBS

A Textile Cone pokes out its siphon as it moves

A Textile Cone burrowing into sand

There are more than 500 species of cones. Northern Australia has a large number of species, and more than a dozen sorts of cones are found in southern waters. Cones are predators. Most feed on worms and other molluscs, and a few kill and eat small fish. A cone has a sac in its snout, or proboscis, which stores venom. Its radula consists of hollow barbed shafts, like tiny harpoons. Around 20 shafts are held in storage; these shafts can be filled with venom when needed. The proboscis can stretch out of the cone's shell for a distance equal to the shell's length. It feels around and when it touches the prey fires a barb into it. The paralysed prey is pulled in, the cone's body envelops it, and it is swallowed whole.

FACTS

▶ Gastropods may be male, female or hermaphrodite. When gastropods which have separate sexes mate, sperm is placed in the female's reproductive opening. She lays eggs in protective capsules which contain yolk to feed the embryos.

▶ Young gastropods may leave the egg capsule as free-swimming planktonic larvae, which eventually settle and become adults. Alternatively, they may hatch as tiny adults.

▶ Some gastropods change sex during their lifetime.

▶ Female Baler Shells are larger than males of the same species, and have been seen eating them.

▶ A human harpooned by a cone suffers paralysis and breathing problems. The Geographer Cone has been held responsible for 12 deaths, the Textile Cone for two. No live cone should be handled. Anyone stung by a cone should seek medical help as soon as possible.

Gastropod shells

Spider shell

Murex shell

Cone shell

Stromb shell

Turban shell

Sundial shell

Spiders and strombs live on shallow coral reefs, in sand and amongst coral. They feed on algae. Male and female shells may have different shaped spines and different coloured shell openings. **Murex** live on shallow reefs and amongst intertidal rocks. They feed on barnacles and molluscs. Their mantle edges form folds and tucks which are protected by spines along the edge of the shell. **Cones** live on sandy sea floors and under boulders. They feed on molluscs, worms and fishes. **Turbans** crawl around on shallow reefs, where they feed on algae and organic debris. **Sundials** occur in tropical and temperate seas. Their flattened, spiral shells often wash up on beaches.

Auger shell

Volute shell

Cowrie shells

Mitre shell

Murex shell

Tun shells

Augers *bury themselves in clean sand. They feed on small invertebrates, usually marine worms, and some species have a poison gland (which is harmless to humans) and harpoon-like radula.* **Volutes** *live in sand and feed on other gastropods and invertebrates. Australia has about 70 species.* **Cowries** *feed at night. Some eat algae, spindle cowries eat gorgonians and egg cowries eat coelenterates.* **Mitres** *live among corals or burrow in sand in tropical and temperate waters. They are predators, or scavenge dead animals. When touched, a mitre may produce evil-smelling purple fluid.* **Tuns** *have no operculum, and hide by burrowing in sand. They are usually found in deeper water.*

- The name nudibranch means "naked gills". Another name is "sea slugs".

- Some nudibranchs wear their gills on their backs, pulling them into special pockets if alarmed.

- Nudibranchs are hermaphrodites and a mating pair exchanges sperm. These may be stored for weeks before they are used to fertilise eggs, which are laid on a favoured food.

- A nudibranch larva swims free and does not change into an adult unless it meets a suitable surface with opportunities to feed.

- Once a fish nibbles a nasty-tasting nudibranch, it is not likely to taste other creatures which resemble it.

NUDIBRANCHS

Nudibranchs are often striking in appearance, and may crawl or swim around the sea floor or reef without much effort at concealment. To the human observer, this means many species are easy to watch. To a would-be predator it means that they are probably nasty-tasting and possibly toxic to eat.

As a larva, a nudibranch may possess a shell, but as an adult it is without one. Its flesh may be toxic, due to chemicals made within its body. Some species are brilliantly coloured, others are camouflaged. One group of nudibranchs feeds on coral polyps, hydroids and other stinging coelenterates. They take the nematocysts of their prey and store them in the tips of the feathery or finger-like projections on their backs. Any animal trying to eat such a nudibranch receives a battery of stings from these stolen weapons.

Most nudibranchs favour special diets. Some species eat only one sort of sponge

Bennett's Nudibranch wears brilliant colours

A nudibranch feeding on a stinging hydroid

Two fragile nudibranchs make contact before mating

One group of nudibranchs bears lumpy ridges

This nudibranch's colour may signal that it tastes nasty

Bubbly beauties

The bubble shells are placed in the mollusc group that includes the nudibranchs. They have retained their shells, but a bubble shell animal is too large for its fragile case and cannot withdraw within it for protection.

The head of a bubble shell animal is a flattened shield, which is used for burrowing into soft sand. Most bubble shells specialise in eating worms, but some eat molluscs, including other bubble shells.

The Rose Petal Bubble Shell's shell may be 3 cm in length

Sea hares

Sea hares are molluscs with small, flattened internal shells. The foot is large and muscular, and a large flap encloses the mantle on each side. This flap is waved up and down to help propel the sea hare through the water. Many species are camouflaged in dull browns and greens, and may be overlooked as they feed on algae. If disturbed, they may jet out purple ink.

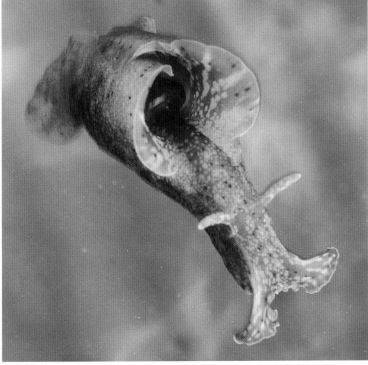
This sea hare's fleshy swimming lobes are at the top of their stroke

Portrait of a sea hare

FACTS

▶ Cephalopods include the Giant Squid, which may measure 20 m to the ends of its tentacles.

▶ The eye of a 12 m long Giant Squid is 40 cm across.

Blushing cuttle

▶ Cephalopods feed on fish and crustaceans. Octopuses also eat bivalve molluscs.

▶ The internal skeleton of a squid is a thin plastic-like structure called the gladius. The octopus has no hard parts except for its powerful, parrot-like beak.

CEPHALOPODS

Cephalopod means "head-and-foot animal". In octopuses, squids, cuttles and their relatives the "foot" common to molluscs has become tentacles, while the head takes on great importance, for cephalopods have the most advanced nervous systems of all invertebrates. Worldwide, there are around 650 species. All live in salt water, and all are active carnivores.

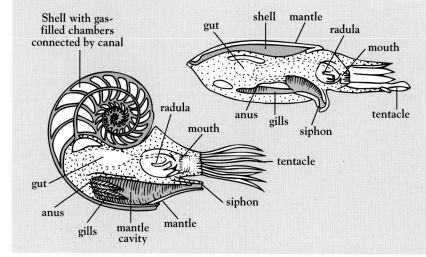

The Giant Cuttle may grow to 1 m in length. It catches prey with two long fishing tentacles, then bites it with its horny beak and rasps it into pieces with its radula

Squids are noted for their rapid colour changes

A cuttle has ten arms and a chalky internal shell

Lots of nerve

Modern cephalopods include nautiluses, cuttles, squids and octopuses.

These animals react quickly to changes in their surroundings because they have giant nerve fibres with few junctions, so messages pass quickly to and from their brains. Their eyes are well developed and compared to other molluscs they have efficient blood systems, with arteries, veins and several hearts. All cephalopods except nautiluses have an ink sac opening off the end of the gut, or digestive canal. Ink is discharged to confuse enemies. Cephalopods can also change their skin colours rapidly and dramatically.

A pair of courting cuttles

Body plans of a primitive* cephalopod, the nautilus (left), and a squid

Diagram labels (nautilus): Shell with gas-filled chambers connected by canal · radula · mouth · gut · anus · gills · mantle cavity · mantle · siphon

Diagram labels (squid): gut · shell · mantle · radula · mouth · anus · gills · siphon · tentacle

An octopus camouflaged to resemble seaweed

A broken Pearly Nautilus shell on the beach

The Pearly Nautilus, which may have 90 tentacles, spends daytime at depths below 200 metres. A nautilus shell ends in numerous chambers containing nitrogen and argon gases. At night the animal increases the amount of gas in the chambers and rises to the surface to feed.

This octopus has turned pale with fear

The jet set

Cuttles and squids have eight shorter arms and two longer tentacles. A cuttle has a flattened body and a spongy internal shell, which is often found washed up on the beach. It is usually solitary, moving slowly around the sea floor. A squid is torpedo-shaped and adapted for fast swimming. It hunts for fish with other squids. An octopus has eight arms and often lives in a crevice or other den. All three creatures propel themselves through the water by jetting water from the mantle cavity through a siphon.

A PALER SHADE WITH FEAR

A sand-dwelling octopus hunting shrimps at night, its body flushed with colour

The same octopus, after seeing danger, loses colour, flattens its body and hastily jets away

FACTS

▶ A male cephalopod uses a special tentacle to place a packet of sperm inside a female's mantle cavity. The eggs are fertilised later, when they are laid.

▶ Cephalopod ink, or sepia, was once used by artists. The blob squirted through the siphon by an alarmed cephalopod has a strong smell and resembles the squirter.

▶ The bite of a Blue-ringed Octopus (above) causes paralysis and breathing problems. This octopus flushes orange and bright blue when agitated.

▶ The two long arms of a cuttle or squid have suckers only on their club-like ends.

▶ Many cephalopods change colour to escape enemies, hide when hunting, or show emotion. The skin contains small, elastic bags of colour, which shrink and expand to pale or colour the animal.

Spined skins, tubed feet

This sea star has added many new legs by regrowth

The echinoderm group includes sea stars, brittle stars, feather stars, sea urchins and sea cucumbers. The skins of these creatures are filled with hard plates or spines and most have the body divided into five radial parts, each with duplicate internal organs. An echinoderm moves on hundreds of tiny hollow tubes, which are lengthened by having sea water pumped into them. Members of this group can regrow lost body parts and some can grow a fragment into a new individual.

SEA STARS

Upper surface of a sea star, showing central anus

Under surface, showing mouth and tube feet

The anus of a sea star is in the centre of its upper side, and its mouth opens at the centre of the underside. The tube feet, which mostly end in suckers, are set in grooves along the undersides of the arms.

The images across the bottom of these two pages show eight variations on the basic five-armed sea star body shape

44

The Southern Sand Star may measure 1 m across. At night, it hunts bivalves, other sea stars and brittle stars

BRITTLE STARS

A brittle star "walks" along on its arms

A brittle star which lives on soft coral

Brittle stars have only one set of internal organs, situated in the central disc. There is a mouth on the underside of the disc, but no anus. The flexible arms are made of limy rings held together with muscle-like tissue.

FACTS

▶ The tube feet of a brittle star lack adhesive suckers. Some produce slimy mucus which traps tiny organisms, so the arms can be used to filter plankton from the current.

▶ A brittle star may shovel mud or sand into its mouth, which is armed with tiny limy teeth. Animal and vegetable content are digested.

▶ Brittle stars escape attackers by shedding their arms, which then regrow.

▶ A brittle star swims by rowing with its arms. Compared to a sea star it is a speedy mover.

▶ Basket stars, which have multi-branched arms, and serpent stars, which often coil around the branches of gorgonians, are specialised forms of brittle stars.

<table>
<tr><td>

DID YOU KNOW?

FACTS

▶ Feather stars are remote survivors of sea lilies which grew up to 15 m in length in the seas 500 million years ago.

</td></tr>
</table>

Feathery food-traps

Feather stars have between five and 200 arms spreading from a central disc. Each arm has many fine, feathery branches. After floating food is caught on a branch, tiny hairs brush it down the centre of the arm to the mouth on the upper side of the disc. A feather star may crawl on appendages called cirri, normally used to cling to a solid surface, or it may swim by flapping its arms.

A feather star with relaxed arms

The underside of a feather star

A Robust Feather Star, showing its anchoring cirri and many feathery arms

SEA CUCUMBERS

Sea cucumbers lie on their sides, using their tentacles to pick up sand and pass it to their mouths. Their skin may be thin, or thick and leathery, and they move by squeezing up then stretching out their bodies. When attacked, some disgorge sticky white threads or their intestines. Some species, bêche-de-mer or trepang, are used in Asian cooking.

A sea cucumber's mouth and tentacles

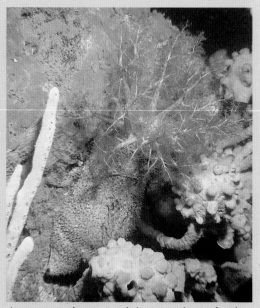

A sea cucumber extends its tentacles to feed

This sea urchin's five rays can be clearly seen

The sand dollar feeds on plankton

Sea urchins

A sea urchin has a five-plated shell, called a test, which is covered with thin skin and carrie movable spines.

Long, thin tube feet protrude from channels between the plates. The tube feet are used for movement, helped by leverage from the spines on the underside of the body.

Sea urchins eat algae and encrusting organisms such as sponges. The mouth is set in the middle of the underside of the body and contains a set of jaws and horny teeth which was named "Aristotle's lantern" over 2000 years ago.

A live sea urchin hides under the test of a dead one

Ijima's Sea Urchin has venomous pedicellariae

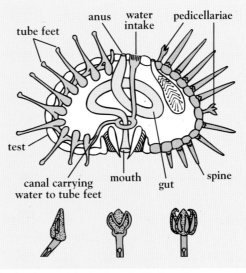

anus   water intake   pedicellariae
tube feet
test
canal carrying water to tube feet   mouth   gut   spine

Body plan and typical pedicellariae of a sea urchin

Moss animals

A bryozoan colony is made up of individuals called zooids, all of which are descended by division from one founder parent.

In many colonies, all zooids are similar and all take part in feeding and sexual reproduction. Each lives in a cup with horny or limy walls. Each individual has a feeding crown of hollow tentacles, with a central mouth leading into a gut. Wastes pass out through an anus outside the circle of tentacles. Colony members are independent of each other, but all retract as one when disturbed.

FACTS

▸ Bryozoans existed 500 million years ago.

▸ Bryozoans live on rock or coral walls, under stones and on boats and jetties.

▸ Colony members shed eggs and sperm, which unite to form free-swimming larvae. When a larva attaches to a solid object, it divides and begins a new colony.

▸ Bryozoans filter food from the water. In some advanced bryozoans, some zooids are supplied with food by others. They have jaws which protect the colony against small predators, or bristles which brush it clear of sediment.

A colony of bryozoans, or moss animals

A bryozoan colony is a refuge for a feather star

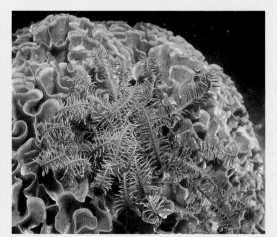

The feather star crawls over the bryozoan colony

A mixed colony of invertebrates on a coral reef contains many bryozoans

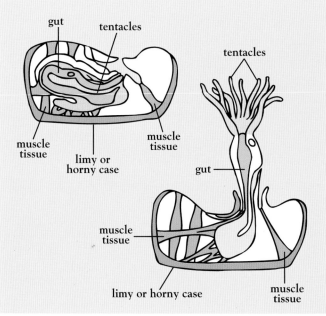

A single bryozoan zooid, withdrawn (top) and extended (above)

gut tentacles muscle tissue muscle tissue limy or horny case tentacles gut muscle tissue limy or horny case muscle tissue

The Brain Ascidian grows to 200 mm across

The Magnificent Ascidian occurs in southern waters

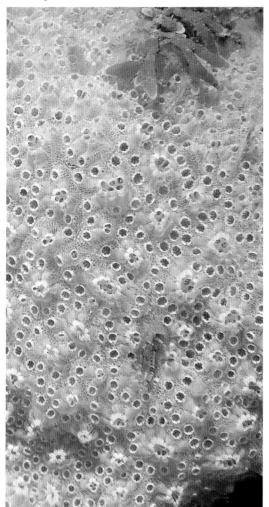

A colony of ascidians

Sea squirts

The adult ascidian, or sea squirt, is a sac with two openings, one for water to enter, the other for it to exit. Its outer covering is surrounded by a fibrous tunic and it may be solitary, or one zooid in a colony of many.

Sea squirts produce larvae which are like tadpoles. They have a notochord, a rod like that which supports the bodies of embryonic vertebrates, and holes where the gill-slits are in fishes. An adult has no notochord.

Colonial ascidians

The Red Sea Squirt is a solitary ascidian

FACTS

▶ The material enclosing ascidian zooids may have sponges, algae and other ascidians growing on it and may contain green algae.

▶ Water is kept flowing through an ascidian by the beating of tiny hairs lining the gut.

▶ After food is filtered from the water, the current carries wastes and sometimes reproductive cells out of a second opening.

▶ The cunjevoi of rocky shores, which can reach 20 cm in length and up to 12 cm across, is a sea squirt. The same species is found in South Africa and Chile (South America). All three places were once part of the supercontinent Gondwana.

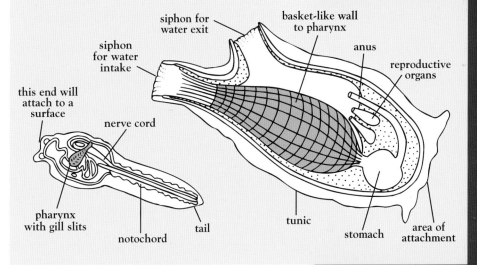

An ascidian larva (left) and adult (right)

DID YOU KNOW?

FACTS

- The Great White Shark (below) has been responsible for human deaths. It is now an endangered species.

- 166 species of sharks and 117 rays are found in Australian waters.

- A shark can smell one part of fish oil or blood in one million parts of sea water.

- The Australian Shark Attack File kept at Taronga Zoo, Sydney, records less than 200 fatal shark attacks around Australian coasts since 1791. Nearly all attacks were made by one of four species, the Great White, Tiger, Bull or Oceanic Whitetip Sharks.

Splendid predators

Fishes are animals which have backbones and are adapted to live in water, breathing through gills and moving with the aid of fins. There are two major groups of fishes, one with skeletons made of cartilage, the other with skeletons made of bone.

A cat shark, showing gill slits and spiracle

The cartilaginous fishes include sharks and rays. Their skeletons are made of cartilage, or gristle, and their skins are covered with small tooth-like scales. Their teeth are not fused to their jaws and are replaced continuously throughout life. Large, oil-filled livers help their bodies remain buoyant in water. Sharks are predators. When hunting, they may use smell, touch, taste, and vision to locate prey. They are also sensitive to changes in water pressure and tiny electrical signals given out by animal bodies. There are over 370 species of sharks worldwide, only one found in fresh water.

Sharks gather in groups of one sex and, usually, one size

A Port Jackson Shark mouths its egg case

Cannibal babies

A male shark or ray has fins which form claspers to place sperm into the female. She may lay eggs protected by horny covers, or the eggs may hatch inside her. Some young sharks hunt down and eat other embryos in the uterus until eventually only one survivor is left to be born.

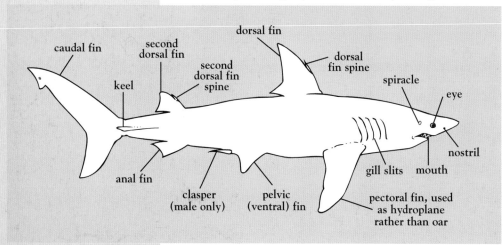
The body plan of a shark

caudal fin
second dorsal fin
keel
second dorsal fin spine
dorsal fin
second dorsal fin spine
dorsal fin spine
spiracle
eye
nostril
mouth
gill slits
pectoral fin, used as hydroplane rather than oar
pelvic (ventral) fin
clasper (male only)
anal fin

A stingaree can produce an electric charge

Body plan of a ray

eye
spiracle
cartilage
thorns
pectoral fin
caudal fin
clasper (male)
pelvic fin
second dorsal fin
stinging spine
first dorsal fin

FACTS

▶ Worldwide, there are more than 4500 species of rays. Most are marine, though some stingrays and sawfishes live in fresh water.

▶ The Manta Ray feeds on plankton filtered through its gills. It may exceed 9 m across the disc and has no stinging spine on its tail.

▶ Toxin from a stingray wound is destroyed by heat. Pain from a wound can be relieved by placing it in hot water.

▶ An electric ray can produce a shock of up to 220 volts.

▶ Most rays bear live young.

Flying discs

Rays probably developed from sharks. Most are flattened and have wing-like pectoral fins which, with the body, form a disc. The tail is whip-like and may carry one or more stinging spines.

Most rays are bottom-dwellers, eating invertebrates and small fishes. A few are scavengers. The group includes sawfishes, which stun and kill prey with their saw-like snouts. Torpedo rays produce electric charges from organs behind their eyes. Stingrays, which may weigh more than 350 kilograms, have venomous barbs on their tails. The devil rays include the Manta Ray, one of the largest living fishes.

A ray swims through coral outcrops

CLINT HEMPSALL

The Manta Ray sucks plankton-rich water through its huge mouth

Compare the sizes of ray and human

MARK SIMMONS

51

FACTS

▶ There are more than 24 000 fish species known to science.

▶ Because of the power needed to move through water, which is 800 times denser than air, swimming muscles make up 40% to 60% of a fish's body weight.

▶ The fastest swimming fishes, such as tuna, have stiff, sickle-like tails which produce thrust but little drag.

▶ The body of a bony fish takes the temperature of the water around it. Some sharks have a heat exchange system which allows them to keep their body temperature above that of the water.

BONY FISHES

Scaled wonders

Bony fishes have skeletons of true bone. Their teeth are usually fused to their jaws. Inside their bodies are gas-filled sacs called swim bladders, which allow them to remain steady in the water at any depth they choose.

Many fishes move by bending their bodies so their tail fins thrust against the water. The body fins are used for swimming, for "walking" across surfaces, to change position in the water, to inject poison, to frighten enemies and even to lure prey.

The scales of a bony fish are partly embedded in the skin. The free parts overlap like tiles on a roof. Patterns and colours serve as camouflage, and help fish to recognise each other. Many fishes can change colour and their colours may become brighter in the breeding season or pale with alarm.

Fish scales overlap and point backward to aid streamlining

Many bony fishes, like this snapper, also called a sea perch, are considered good eating by humans

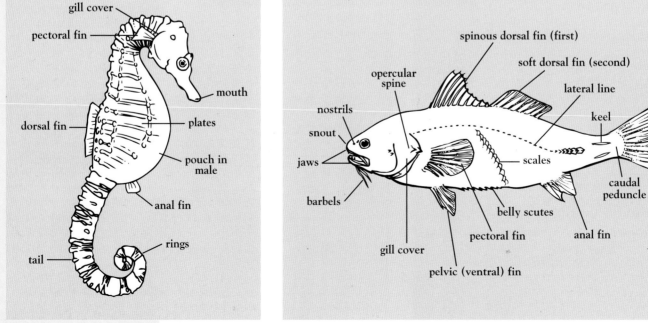

Seahorse

gill cover
pectoral fin
mouth
dorsal fin
plates
pouch in male
anal fin
tail
rings

Bony fish

spinous dorsal fin (first)
soft dorsal fin (second)
opercular spine
lateral line
filament
nostrils
keel
snout
jaws
caudal (tail) fin
barbels
scales
caudal peduncle
belly scutes
pectoral fin
anal fin
gill cover
pelvic (ventral) fin

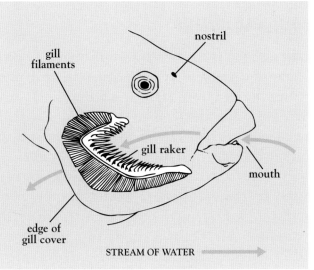

When a mudskipper comes out of the water onto the mud, it breathes oxygen from water it is carrying in its gill chambers

Taking oxygen from water

Water contains around one-thirtieth of the oxygen which exists in air. A fish obtains oxygen by sucking in water through its mouth and forcing it out again through gill slits behind the head. It passes through gill chambers containing gill rakers, which remove solid material, and gill filaments, which take out up to 95 per cent of the oxygen available. Some fish are able to take oxygen from air in their swim bladder.

This fish is taking in water through its mouth. Water is passing out again under its expanded gill covers

LIVING TOGETHER

Some fishes form associations with other sorts of animals. Anemone fishes and some species of oceanic fishes gain protection from the stinging cells of sea anemones and sea jellies. Some gobies live with shrimps – the shrimp maintains the home burrow, while the fish keeps watch and signals when it is safe to bring out debris. Suckerfishes (remoras) use suckers on their heads to attach themselves to large fishes, turtles and dugongs. Certain gobies, butterflyfishes and cleaner wrasses set up cleaner stations, where they swim around larger fishes, nipping off tiny parasites which live on them and in their gill chambers. These cleaners are important to the health of fish communities.

Two cleaner wrasse attending to a Coral Trout

Sensing their surroundings

Fishes live in habitats ranging from shallow sunlit pools to dark ocean depths, and have a variety of sense organs to help them survive. Many groups have good vision, and some fishes, especially those with swim bladders, hear well. Along a fish's side is a lateral line of nerve cells, linked to a network on the head, which perceives even a slight movement in the water.

Many fishes have organs which can detect electrical currents, such as those produced by the swimming muscles of prey. Some navigate great distances guided by a sense of the Earth's magnetic fields. Some fishes produce electricity, using it to communicate with their own species and repel predators as well as to stun prey.

Catfish touch and taste through chin barbels

Making more fishes

The eggs of bony fishes are fertilised outside the female's body. Some groups broadcast eggs and sperm into the ocean, while others prepare nests and take care of their fertilised eggs and sometimes their young.

In some fish families, such as wrasses and parrotfishes, every fish is born female, but may later change sex to male. In some other families, such as anemonefishes, each fish is born male, but may later become female. A female seahorse uses an appendage called an ovipositor* to place her eggs in a male's belly pouch, where they are fertilised and hatch. Some fishes guard breeding and feeding territories, chasing away others of their own species.

A Harlequin Tuskfish begins life as a female, but can turn into a male

An adult Immaculate Damselfish

A juvenile Immaculate Damselfish

An adult reef fish will usually allow a juvenile to remain in its territory while the young fish wears different colours.

Gold-spotted Rabbitfish are seen in pairs

A male Diana's Hogfish guards a harem*

The female Sergeant Baker (above left) and the male (above right) look quite different

54

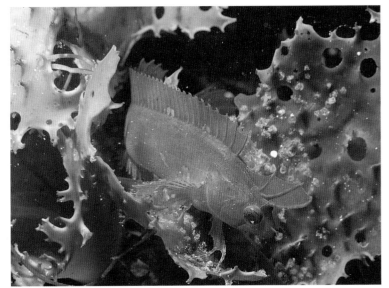

A Golden Weedfish hides amongst fronds of kelp

A Barrier Reef Anemonefish is protected by anemone tentacles

The poisonous Saddled Puffer is imitated by the Mimic Filefish above it

A camouflaged Bridled Leatherjacket erects its dorsal spine

Save yourself if you can

The ocean is full of predators, and fishes protect themselves in many ways. They may hide, or have sharp teeth, or venomous spines, or poisonous flesh, or mimic fish which do have these things. Some use bluff to frighten away attackers, and some form partnerships with more formidable creatures.

The Butterfly Gurnard flashes its fins when alarmed

A porcupinefish can blow up its body so its spines point outwards

A parrotfish sleeps in a mucous cocoon which hides its scent

How fishes live

Coral Cod and Longfin Bannerfish

▶ There may be over 2000 species of fishes living on the Great Barrier Reef, more than half Australia's estimated total of 3 600 species.

▶ Many coral reef fishes live in just one habitat. Some species are territorial and defend their feeding, breeding and sleeping areas against other fish of the same species.

▶ The Trumpetfish changes colour to blend with another fish, then uses it for cover, even sneaking into a cleaning station at its side. When in reach of a victim, it shoots out its expandable jaw and sucks in the prey.

A Trumpetfish can swallow fish almost its own size

Coral reefs grow in warm, clear seas, which lack the nutrients found in colder waters. The partnership between coral polyps and zooxanthellae enables the construction of reefs which provide shelter and food for many lifeforms. These "oases in the ocean desert" house ecosystems* whose richness is rivalled only by tropical rainforest.

A diversity of fishes

An area of coral reef less than one hectare in extent may contain as many as 200 species of fishes, ranging in size from gobies 10 millimetres in length to the Whale Shark 20 metres long. This diversity is possible because the reef offers many ways in which to obtain food.

Moray eels are fish. These two are gulping water to breathe

Shaped like pipes or plates

Coral fishes take many shapes, from elongated pipefishes to ribbon-like eels, torpedo-like barracudas, bull-shouldered groupers and saucer-like angelfishes. Shape is related to a fish's way of life and particularly its way of feeding. The trumpetfish's odd shape allows it to use another fish as a cover when stalking prey. The narrow, saucer bodies and efficient fins of fish which feed on coral polyps or graze on algae allow them to hover, back up or cruise slowly. Active hunters like barracuda are streamlined.

Pipefishes slide over coral, feeding on small creatures

The Ring-tail Cardinalfish belongs to a group which brood their eggs in their mouths

Ornate Butterflyfish (left) and Pinstriped Butterflyfish feed on coral polyps

Colour signals

Bright colours may identify coral fishes, signal their age, advertise their social status, or conceal them amongst the brilliant background of the reef. Many can change colour.

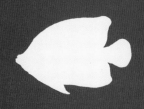

Fishes fishing for fishes

Fishes which eat other fishes have a variety of body mechanisms to make them efficient predators.

Many have jaws which extend out of their mouth, creating a large space which "vacuums" up anything in the water in front of it. In the throat is a second set of jaws, which crush any hard material in the mouthful. Special glands produce mucus which lines the throat so roughage passes down easily.

Some fish-eaters hunt down their prey in the open, but others lurk in ambush, often well camouflaged. When a victim swims near, the hunter opens its enormous mouth and gulps it down.

Nightlife

Most fishes are active during daytime, but some groups are night feeders. Bigeyes, cardinalfishes and squirrelfishes shelter in caves and under ledges. They may form large resting groups during the day and spread out at night to feed.

Crescent-tail Bigeye

Tailspot Squirrelfish

Anglerfish lure victims close with a "rod" and "bait" made of dorsal spines. The "bait" mimics some creature eaten by the target prey

The Leaf Scorpionfish, or Paperfish, sits on coral waiting for prey

FACTS

▶ All pufferfishes have toxins in their skins and often in their internal organs. Many have spiny skins and can inflate their bodies.

▶ A pufferfish can "sweat" poison into the water around it when threatened.

▶ Japanese and Korean diners have been killed by eating the flesh and reproductive organs of *Takifugu* pufferfish, which may contain a nerve poison stronger than cyanide.

Black-spot Snapper shelter in coral caves during the day and venture out to feed at night

Solo or ensemble

Many fish find safety in numbers: many eyes watch for predators and most escape while one is taken. Predators which take victims from ambush often live alone. The most visible fish on a coral reef may be those with defences such as poisonous flesh or venomous spines.

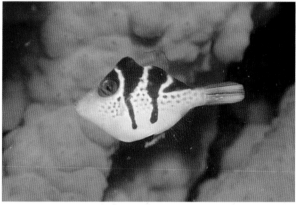

The Mimic Filefish bluffs its way past possible predators by imitating the venomous Saddled Puffer

Black-spot Goatfish are found in groups. They may change colour suddenly

A porcupinefish is confident in its armour of spines

Each of these Blue-stripe Snapper is keeping watch

58

The Variegated Lizardfish is a large-mouthed predator which ambushes other fishes and is usually found alone

Fishy sounds

The ocean is full of animal noises. Fish produce sounds by swimming, by rubbing together two bony parts of the body, such as teeth or spines, or by quickly contracting their swim bladders.

They hear with their ears, but they also detect vibrations with their lateral lines. Unlike a human diver, a fish can tell which direction a sound is coming from.

Fish use noise to warn intruders off their territories, for courtship and to detect predators or likely prey. Fish noises, like birdsong, peak at dawn and dusk.

A male damselfish responds to the chirps made by females of his own species and ignores noises made by females of other species

Predators such as these barracudas are attracted by the distinctive swimming sounds made by their usual prey

Lookalikes

Coral fishes which feed in the same way may resemble each other in shape and colour. The Moorish Idol, which uses its pointed snout to forage in coral, looks like the butterflyfishes and bannerfishes, but is more closely related to the surgeonfishes. These are named because of a scalpel-like spine on each side of the base of the tail. Like a surgeonfish, the Moorish Idol can lock its dorsal spines upright.

Pencilled Surgeonfish

The Moorish Idol resembles a bannerfish, but is related to surgeonfishes

Reef Bannerfish

DID YOU KNOW?

FACTS

▶ Port Jackson Sharks have venom glands which discharge through a spine on each dorsal fin.

▶ An angelshark looks like a ray, but its fins do not extend to its head. It buries itself in sand when not active.

▶ When an angelshark swallows a squid, ink pours from its gill slits.

▶ Captain Cook originally named Botany Bay "Stingray Bay" because of huge rays seen there.

▶ Aborigines used stingray barbs to tip their spears.

▶ The upper surface of an electric ray's body is positive, the underside is negative. The ray may deliver 50 charges within 10 minutes, each strong enough to cramp the muscles of an adult human.

The Port Jackson Shark is a bottom-dweller which feeds on echinoderms and other invertebrates

Fishes which live on the sea floor often have flattened bodies and may spend much time concealed under sand, mud or algae. They may root through the bottom debris seeking food, or ambush unwary victims. Sharks and rays have no swim bladders and many groups find sea floor living convenient. They have developed flattened shapes and are often camouflaged in dull, sandy, muddy colours.

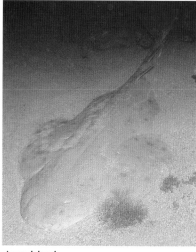

Angelshark

The Eastern Shovelnose Ray lives on sandflats and in seagrass beds

A variety of rays

Shovelnose rays have long, broad, flattened tails without stinging spines. They feed on molluscs, and include fiddler rays which are named because of their shape and scroll-like patterns.

Torpedo, or electric, rays produce electric charges of up to 220 volts; numbfishes are small electric rays. Stingrays have one or more saw-edged stinging spines on the long tail, and stingarees look like stingrays with short tails.

The Eastern Fiddler Ray occasionally enters estuaries

The Numbfish grows to 60 cm in length

Like all catfishes, the Estuary Catfish has a leathery skin and no scales. Its spines can inflict a painful wound

FACTS

▶ Catfishes have thread-like barbels around the mouth. These are used to taste as well as to feel.

▶ A catfish has thorny spines at the front edges of dorsal and pectoral fins. These can be locked erect and in some species deliver venom into a wound.

▶ The largest catfish in the world, the freshwater European Wels, may grow to 5 m and weigh 300 kg.

▶ Australia's marine catfishes have eel-like, tapering tails and 5 pairs of barbels.

▶ A frogfish uses its fins to walk across the bottom. Related to the anglerfishes, it can engulf a victim in less than one-hundredth of a second.

The Eastern Frogfish can change colour to match its background. It bears a fleshy "bait" which lures prey

The Rough Flutemouth may grow to 2 m in length. It hunts small fishes and usually occurs in deep water

FACTS

▶ The venom of the scorpionfish group causes numbness and pain to humans. It is inactivated by heat, so in case of a sting the affected area should be placed in hot water or treated with hot air or sand.

▶ The skin of a stonefish produces sticky fluid. Algae and mud cling to this and the fish may also provide a home for a sea anemone.

A scorpionfish concealed in sand and algae

A stonefish has 13 dorsal spines and 26 poison glands

The sting's in the fins

Scorpionfishes and their relatives, which include the stonefish, cobblers, rockcods, paperfish and lionfishes, are usually less than 30 centimetres in length. They have a bony strut across each cheek, connecting the bone under the eye with the gill cover, which often carries head spines.

Most members of this group of fishes live on the bottom in shallow water, feeding on crustaceans and fishes. Each dorsal spine has a venom gland at its base; when the spine stabs into something, venom is forced into the wound. Stonefishes and scorpionfishes lie concealed on the bottom, waiting for prey. Their spines may remain folded until they feel threatened. Lionfishes are more active and may use their spectacular feathery fins to round up a victim. As the hunter pounces, its mouth and gill covers open, the floor of its mouth drops and the food is vacuumed in.

Eastern Spiny Gurnard has large pectoral fins, used for walking and probing sand. They may be flashed to discourage a predator

Sand-stirring goatfishes

Fish which live on the sea floor often probe in sand or mud for food. Goatfishes have a pair of feelers, or barbels, on their chins.

These barbels are covered with tiny sense organs, like taste buds, which detect small invertebrate animals and other food as the goatfish swims above the sand, digs into it with its teeth or stirs it up with its pectoral fins. Some small wrasses hover around a digging goatfish, waiting to snap up morsels of food.

Blue-lined Goatfish stirring up sand in search of food

White-streaked Grubfish

Black-spotted Sand Goby

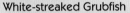

Sand Flathead

Dragonet

The sea floor dwellers

Fishes which live on the mud or sand of the sea floor often have a flattened body camouflaged in mottled, neutral colours. The bulging eyes are on the top of the head, so the fish can lie buried but still detect prey or predator. Many are ambush hunters, which engulf unwary prey in their huge mouth. Their young may swim at the surface for a time before adopting adult habits.

Eastern Stargazer sucks prey into its huge mouth

Flat soles

Soles have both their eyes on one side of the body. The other side lacks colour and is used as the underside. A sole spends much time buried, and feeds on invertebrates or fishes taken from, or just above, the sea floor.

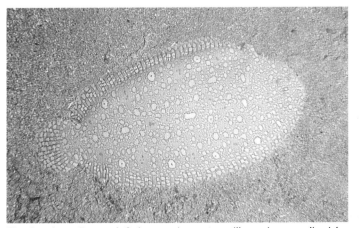
The Southern Peacock Sole can give out a milky poisonous liquid

FACTS

▶ Gobies are the largest family of marine fishes and Australia has about 350 species. They may partner with shrimps or other creatures.

▶ Dragonets have tough, mucus-covered skin instead of scales. Because of their strong smell they may be called "stinkfish".

▶ Flatheads have flattened heads, often carrying large spines. Some species lack swim bladders and live on the sea floor.

▶ A stargazer has a fleshy tag in its mouth. This is wriggled to attract fish, which are sucked in whole. The large backward-pointing spine above the base of each pectoral fin may be venomous.

▶ A sole larva has eyes on both sides of its head. After a while, one eye travels across the top of the head to the other side of the body. The adult sole lies on the sea floor on its "blind" side.

▶ in 1960, two scientists in a bathyscaphe (a submersible), saw a sole lying on the floor of the Mariana Trench, at 10 933 m deep.

DID YOU KNOW?

FACTS

▶ The Green Moray's unusual colour is caused by algae cells in its skin tissue. Sunlight influences plant growth, so the greenest eels are from the shallowest water.

▶ The Golden Roughy, which is known only from Topgallant Island in the Great Australian Bight, makes loud noises like rapidly hitting a cup with a spoon.

Rocky coasts offer many habitats for fishes of all sorts. The rock platforms of the intertidal zone harbour species which can survive the continual surge and backflow of the waves. Over the edge of these platforms, rocks and reefs provide caves and crevices for shelter and a wealth of marine life to feed larger fishes. Once the water temperature falls below 17.5°C, coral gives way to rock and the fish population includes more temperate species.

The Green Moray Eel is common in rocky habitats

Pineapplefish have heavy body armour of plate-like scales

Headlights

On either side of its lower jaw, a Pineapplefish has a patch of skin which carries a colony of luminous bacteria. This area appears orange during the day and glows blue-green at night. The fish hides in caves during day and uses the light at night to locate the shrimps on which it feeds.

Slender Roughy

Roughy

Roughies

Roughies are rocky reef dwellers with deep, narrow bodies and keel-edged scales along the abdomen. Some make loud buzzing or clicking sounds. The Orange Roughy is trawled for human use.

The Red Rockcod is a venomous relative of the lionfishes

Threefins take on the colour of their surroundings, often matching sponges

Male and female Splendid Perch

Weedy Seadragon eggs are carried on the male's tail

Weedy Seadragon

Seahorses, seadragons and pipefishes have bodies protected by bony plates and long snouts ending in tiny, toothless mouths. The females pass their eggs to the males, which then incubate* them. Seahorses protect them in a pouch, while seadragons carry up to 250 eggs stuck to their bodies or tails.

The Big-belly Seahorse may grow to 30 cm in length

FACTS

▶ Most species of seahorse live in pairs.

▶ Seahorse eggs are fertilised in the male's pouch. The lining of the pouch then provides nourishment for the developing eggs.

▶ Seahorses, seadragons and pipefishes feed on tiny drifting animals. Their long snouts act like pipettes, sucking in water and prey.

Caring males

Hulafish males guard and protect their egg clusters by wrapping their bodies around the holes that contain them. Cardinalfish males incubate their eggs, then carry their fry in their mouths.

Eastern Hulafish feed on plankton above coastal rocky reefs

Juvenile Striped Catfish school on a reef

The Largetooth Beardy uses ventral fins as feelers

▶ Males of most damselfishes, anemonefishes, gobies and triggerfishes tend their nests of fertilised eggs. A cardinalfish male may keep as many as 20 000 tiny eggs in his throat, turning them constantly. Some catfishes are also mouth brooders.

FACTS

▸ Worldwide, there are about 670 species of wrasses and parrotfishes. Australian waters are home to about half these.

▸ The Western Blue Grouper grows to about 1.6 m in length and may weigh over 30 kg. The largest non-Australian wrasse grows to 2.5 m and weighs nearly 200 kg.

▸ The wrasses include several species which act as fish cleaners.

▸ The difference in colour between male and female wrasses of some kinds may be so great that they were once thought to be different species.

▸ A male wrasse in juvenile colours may sneak unchallenged into a dominant male's territory. He will follow the male and an egg-full female and as they spawn will release his own sperm in an attempt to fertilise the eggs.

FROM HER TO HIM

Blue Grouper

Circle-cheek Wrasse

Maori Wrasse

Yellow Moon Wrasse

Wrasses are found in tropical and temperate waters, and feed on plankton, invertebrates or small fish. Juvenile, mature female and mature male wrasses often have different colour patterns and juveniles are usually female. A mature male guards a harem of females. If he disappears, the largest female in the harem changes sex within a few days and takes over his role as dominant male.

Morwongs

Morwongs are eaten by humans and have thick, rubbery lips, long pectoral fins and forked tails. They gobble mouthfuls of sand and filter it through their gill rakers, retaining and swallowing worms and molluscs.

Blue Morwong

The Old Wife, or Zebrafish, is found only in Australian waters. It has a venomous dorsal spine and swims in large schools

Wobbegong

There are seven species of wobbegong, all occurring in Australian waters. They are flattened bottom-dwellers which are more athletic than they look. Wobbegongs hunt cephalopods and crustaceans at night. They attack their prey vigorously, screwing up their bodies and twisting as they tear the prey apart.

This resting Banded Wobbegong could bite its own tail

Boxed in by armour

A boxfish has a protective covering of large, thick, joined scale plates. This hard covering makes the boxfish safe from any predator which does not have an enormous mouth. Some boxfishes also produce a poisonous substance which can be released into the surrounding water.

Cowfishes are tropical boxfishes which have long spines in front of the eyes. Their bony armour has a hole for each moving part – fins, gills, eyes and mouth.

Thorny-back Cowfish

FACTS

▶ Boxfish cannot bend their bodies to swim or hunt. They "stand on their heads" and blow away sand to expose prey, then suck it up through tube-like lips.

▶ Armoured fishes first swam in the world's oceans more than 245 million years ago.

Smooth Boxfish

SWIVEL-HIPS

Leatherjackets have a ball and socket mechanism which locks the first dorsal spine erect. They also have a pelvic bone which can be swivelled downward, stretching the skin between pelvis and anus and making the body look larger. If this does not discourage a predator, the leatherjacket darts into a crevice in the reef, erects the dorsal spine, swivels its pelvis and wedges itself securely into its refuge.

Six-spine Leatherjacket

Mosaic Leatherjacket

▶ Some of the oceanic tunas and sharks are able to raise their blood temperature and muscle efficiency.

▶ Many predatory pelagic fishes hunt in groups, attacking a school of prey and panicking individuals so they break formation and are captured.

▶ Over the past 10 years, world catches of tuna, mackerel and bonita have been between 5 and 6 million tonnes each year.

IN THE OPEN OCEAN

There is no place to hide in the surface layers of the open ocean. The pelagic* fishes which live here are fast-swimming athletes which escape danger by bursts of speed. Many are schooling fish, finding added safety in numbers. As well, most have protective coloration, blue or dark grey on top and silvery underneath, making them less visible to predators above or below them.

The larvae of many fishes look very different from their parents. After hatching, they spend some time living in the ocean's surface water, where planktonic food is abundant.

Pelagic fishes are an important source of food for humans. They may be fished commercially or for sport.

Anchovies, or sprats, filter-feed on plankton as they swim

Longfin Pike is found in schools in clear oceanic waters or offshore near reefs

Trevally are streamlined, fast swimmers which hunt small fishes

Hardyheads are an important food source for pelagic fishes

KELVIN AITKEN

FACTS

▶ The fastest sharks are probably the makos, which can leap repeatedly from the water. This requires a swimming speed of 35 km/h.

▶ A sailfish has been timed swimming in excess of 110 km/h for short periods.

▶ The sword-like beak of an adult billfish is an extension of the upper jaw. The beak is used to stun other fishes, which are then seized in toothless jaws.

▶ The ocean sunfishes are huge, disc-shaped, pelagic fishes which may reach 3 m in length and 2 tonnes in weight. They feed on sea jellies and other soft-bodied invertebrates.

Some shark attacks on humans result from mistaken identity. A shark may mistake a swimmer in a wetsuit for a seal or a dolphin. Most sharks prefer to swim away from divers, but may attack if they feel threatened. Nearly all attacks can be attributed to one of four species: the Great White Shark (above) in cooler water, Tiger and Bull Sharks in warmer, shallow water and estuaries, and the Oceanic Whitetip in the open ocean.

Bigeye Trevally show the typical streamlined shape of fishes which swim fast to catch other fishes

Billfishes

The billfishes include the swordfish, sailfish and marlin, most of which are popular sport fishes. The Indo-Pacific Sailfish, which is found off the Pilbara coast of Western Australia and north of Moreton Bay, Queensland, has become a target for anglers in small craft. The Australian game-fishing record for a sailfish is 55.79 kilograms, while the world record is 100.24 kilograms. Happily, most sailfish caught these days are tagged and released.

The Indo-pacific Sailfish has no teeth and stuns prey with its sword-like bill

69

DID YOU KNOW?

FACTS

▶ Leatherback Turtles have been recorded diving to depths over 1000 m.

▶ Glands beside a turtle's tear ducts pass excess salt out of its body.

▶ A marine turtle "flies" through the water, using its front flippers like wings.

Reptilian mariners

Reptiles are animals whose bodies take the temperature of their surroundings. They may have four limbs, or two, or none, and their bodies are covered with scales.

Australia's oceans are home to marine turtles and seasnakes. The Saltwater Crocodile may be found in estuaries and occasionally out to sea. However, there are no species of marine lizards in Australian waters.

A Green Turtle swimming, showing its horny beak and shell

Endangered turtles

The world has six species of marine turtles. The Loggerhead, Flatback, Green, Hawksbill and Leatherback are considered endangered. The Olive Ridley is plentiful in some seas. All nest on Australian coasts.

Between November and February, females drag themselves up onto beaches to dig nest pits and lay eggs. They return to the sea and warm sands incubate the eggs. Hatchlings emerge from January to April. Perhaps one in 100 will survive to breed in future years.

MARK SIMMONS

Green Turtles mating. The female is carrying two sucker fish, or remoras

A Green Turtle laboriously digs a nest pit into beach sand

Eggs are laid in a chamber

The turtle returns to the sea

Snakes of the sea

Seasnakes live in warm tropical and subtropical seas, often in coastal waters. They may grow up to two metres, and their tails are upright paddles.

Olive Seasnake

Some species have small, non-overlapping scales, others have overlapping scales and some bear spines or ridged scales. Their nostrils, which are on the top of the snout, can be closed when under water. Seasnakes breathe air, but may also take in oxygen through their skins. A gland under the tongue removes excess salt from the bloodstream and passes it out of the body.

Seasnakes eat fishes and fish eggs. They have fangs and powerful venom and though they are not aggressive their bite is potentially dangerous.

An Olive Seasnake swallowing an eel – the snake's head is at the top of the picture

SALTWATER CROCODILE

The Saltwater Crocodile, also called the Estuarine Crocodile, may reach seven metres in length and weigh over one tonne. This reptile breeds in tidal rivers around Australia's north. Some males have territories which stretch along the sea coast and individuals may be seen well out to sea.

Ocean fliers

The Osprey is a bird of prey which eats fish and may be seen anywhere on the Australian coast

Birds are vertebrates which make their own body heat and the front two limbs of which have become wings. Their bodies are covered with feathers and their legs are protected by scales. Although many sorts of birds find food in the ocean and around its shores, they all need to come to land to breed, on islands, on seashores or in dune vegetation.

Some sea birds, such as albatrosses and petrels, spend most of their lives above or on the ocean, and touch down on land only to nest. Others, like terns, roost on land each night and fly to sea at dawn to find food. Shore birds find food on beaches and mudflats.

The giant-petrels are tube-nosed sea birds.

JIRI LOCHMAN

Tube-nosed sea birds, such as albatrosses, petrels and shearwaters, have long, plated bills with tube-like nostrils. They feed on surface squid and fishes, or filter plankton from the waves, and they nest on islands, many in burrows.

Oystercatchers feed on sandy or stony beaches. They probe the beach with their chisel beaks and, when they find a cockle or other bivalve, prise the shells apart and eat the mollusc inside.

The Eastern Reef Egret is only found on the coast, where it fishes the intertidal zone

Pair of Pied Oystercatchers

Living off the sea

Sea birds eat fish, squid and other marine creatures, catching them in various ways.

Pelicans scoop fish from the surface, gannets and boobies plunge-dive then swim with feet and wings after prey. Terns spear fishes with their sharp bills, while gulls gobble any live, or dead, food they can handle. Frigatebirds' speciality is attacking other birds carrying fish back to their chicks and forcing them to drop their catch, which is seized and eaten.

A Masked Booby displays a fish-catching gape

Terns hover above the sea, plunging to catch fish

Frigatebirds pirate fish from other sea birds

These Crested Terns are nesting on a coral cay, where space is limited so that nests are a beak-length apart

Flying through water

Penguins "fly" through the sea. Their wings have become stiff, narrow flippers lacking the flight feathers of airborne birds. Their body feathers are short and stiff, covering thick down which traps air so they lose little body heat. Their short legs, set far back on their bodies, end in webbed feet. The Little Penguin is the only species to breed in Australia. Pairs come ashore through spring and summer, to nest in rock crevices or sand burrows and provide "penguin parades" for human observers.

The Little Penguin nests around southern coasts

FACTS

▶ The Masked Booby may plunge-dive for fish from a height of 100 m.

▶ Petrels and shearwaters are magnificent fliers, but are clumsy walkers as their legs are set well back. When nesting, they land at night to evade predators.

▶ Each year, the Short-tailed Shearwater breeds around southern Australian coasts, then flies to the North Pacific.

▶ Approximately 60 species of shore birds feed on Australia's coasts during summer. Nearly two-thirds of these migrate to northern Asia during Australia's winter.

▶ More facts in Volume 3 in this series.

Hairy seafarers

FACTS

▶ Australian Fur-seals which look longingly at the salmon being farmed around Tasmanian coasts are trapped by wildlife officers and relocated. The record for most returns is held by "Radar", who turned up at a Port Arthur farm 17 times. Released at Strahan, on the west coast of the island, he took only 5 days to return.

▶ Discover more about marine mammals in Volume 2 in this series.

A female Elephant Seal, showing nostrils which can close underwater and predator's forward-directed eyes

A mammal is a four-limbed vertebrate animal which produces its own body heat. Its skin grows hair and the female feeds the young on milk made in special glands in her body.

Marine mammals have streamlined bodies and limbs adapted for swimming. The only Australian groups able to emerge from the water are the seals and sea-lions, which come to land to breed. A "warm-blooded" animal continually loses body heat in cooler seas. To combat this, marine mammals have thick layers of fat beneath their skin, and seals and sea-lions have a dense coat of fur and hair. Dugongs, dolphins and whales are also true mammals. All have hair, even if it is present only in young animals, or as eyelashes.

Australian Fur-seals swim using their front flippers

A female Australian Sea-lion suckles her large pup

Australian Fur-seals breed on nine islands in Bass Strait. Within six weeks in November and December, females give birth and mate about a week later. Australian Sea-lions occur on islands from Houtman Abrolhos, Western Australia, to Kangaroo Island, South Australia. The population numbers only 3000 to 5000. Both species were the target of sealers in the early nineteenth century; their numbers were drastically reduced, but the fur-seal in particular has slowly repopulated.

Gentle grazers

The Dugong, the only living herbivorous marine mammal, is found around Australia's northern coasts from Shark Bay, Western Australia, to Moreton Bay, Queensland. Its heavy skeleton keeps it on the sea floor as it gathers seagrasses with its broad upper lip. A Dugong may be 15 years old before reproducing. The species is threatened by habitat loss from human development and pollution.

GEOFF TAYLOR

A Dugong swims accompanied by small fish and three hitch-hiking remoras, or suckerfish

Bottlenose Dolphins. The blowhole of one shows clearly

Sociable speedsters

Dolphins are small toothed whales which feed on fishes and cephalopods. They are powerful, fast swimmers which breathe through a blowhole on top of the head. They locate and identify objects by bouncing high-pitched sounds off them and examining the echoes.

Ocean giants

A number of species of whale may be seen close inshore on Australian coasts. Best-known of the larger species are the Humpback and the Southern Right Whale. The Humpback mates and gives birth in the warm waters off northeastern and northwestern Australia before migrating to rich Antarctic feeding grounds.

Two male Humpback Whales breaching, or leaping out of the water

FACTS

▶ When a male Humpback Whale is looking for a female, he produces a song which may be detected underwater up to 185 km away. In one season, all whales in one area sing one song, with slight individual differences.

▶ The Humpback Whale, which may be 16 m long, eats shrimp-like krill. These are strained out of the Antarctic water through up to 400 fringed baleen plates hanging from the roof of its mouth.

▶ Groups of Bottlenose Dolphins come to shallow water and interact with humans at a number of places around Australia's coasts.

The sea and humankind

Hunting sea creatures is one of humankind's oldest ways of obtaining food. The resources of the ocean have in the past seemed limitless.

Today, nations lay claim to the sea for 200 nautical miles from their low tide marks. The rest is classed as international waters, used by all but cared for by few. Marine habitats worldwide are becoming polluted and overfished. However, awareness of the damage done to the seas is growing, some threatened species, such as whales, are the subject of conservation efforts and there are hopeful developments in farming some fishes and molluscs.

Self contained underwater breathing apparatus (scuba) has opened the underwater world to people interested in natural history and adventure

A South Australian crayfisher displays rock lobsters which will probably be exported to the USA or Japan

Fishing today is large scale and mechanised, with fish taken on longlines, by bottom trawling or in trawl or drift nets. The continental shelves cover about one-tenth of the oceans, but 99% of commercial fishing takes place there. The sea is not unlimited in resources or in the power to recover from pollution. When fish stocks cannot replace themselves fast enough, fisheries collapse. Some methods of fishing, such as bottom trawling, are very wasteful, destroying many marine creatures to secure the desired commercial species.

Pressures on the oceans

- The human population of the world increases by 90 million each year, with the biggest increase in coastal areas. Many traditional fisheries have ceased to exist because their stocks are exhausted.
- The oceans have for many years been used as dumping grounds for sewage, which nourishes a few species at the expense of many.
- Chemical dumping increases the level of substances such as mercury, now present in the tissues of many marine animals.
- Oil spills from tankers and offshore oil rig blowouts devastate sea birds, marine mammals and other shallow-water wildlife.
- Pesticides and fertilisers wash into the ocean from the land, or are carried into it by rivers.
- Nuclear particles pollute the ocean through discharge of low-level nuclear wastes, or through fallout from nuclear explosions.
- Commercial fishing kills many non-commercial creatures and may remove an over-fished commercial species.
- Drifting garbage, such as plastic, kills turtles and other creatures.

Tourism is a major industry which puts pressure on popular areas such as the Great Barrier Reef islands

Too much loving?

Many coastal areas, especially those with abundant marine life, are under threat from the very people who want to enjoy their wonders. Marine parks offer magnificent opportunities to observe marine creatures: in them, a balance must be struck between public enjoyment and destructive overuse.

Many years have turned this wreck into a perch for sea birds. Today's wrecks threaten oil spillage

Catch of the day for two fishing enthusiasts

Whale-watching is growing in popularity. Tour operators must respect the rights of the whales they watch

FACTS
ABOUT UNDERSEA EXPLORATION

▶ The diving bell was invented in 1791.

▶ 19th and early 20th century divers wore heavy canvas suits with copper helmets, supplied with air through a hose.

▶ Self contained underwater breathing apparatus (scuba) was invented by Jacques Cousteau and Emile Gagnana in the 1940s.

▶ Very deep water is explored in small, strong submersibles. In 1960, the Trieste carried two men to a depth of 11 km.

▶ The US Navy submersible Alvin carries two crew and with the robot submersible Jason Jr explored the wreck of the Titanic. Jason Jr can film at nearly 4000 m deep.

▶ The sea floor is mapped by bouncing sound waves off the bottom and studying the echoes.

Many marine mammals need human protection to survive

Research gives information which may help save marine turtles

The Grey Nurse Shark is protected after being over-hunted

The ocean was the cradle of life on planet Earth. It is up to humankind to preserve and care for it

Glossary

antenna (plural **antennae**). Slender, sensitive feelers.

anus. The final opening of digestive canal of animal.

appendages. Things attached; used of limbs of arthropods.

bacteria. Microscopic one-celled organisms.

baleen. Fibrous plates hanging from the palates of some whale species, used to filter organisms from sea water.

budding off. Forming new individuals by the division of existing creatures without sexual reproduction.

camouflage. To take on colour and pattern which blends with background and makes animal less visible to predators.

carapace. The shield-like plate covering top and sides of the head and thorax of a crustacean.

carnivores. Animals which kill and eat other animals.

colony (verb **colonise**; adjective **colonial**). A group of animals of the same species living closely together.

commensals. Members of two different species which associate so that one benefits and the other is neither disadvantaged nor advantaged.

compound eyes. Eyes made up of many image-forming elements.

desensitise. To reduce or destroy sensitivity by continued exposure to the thing causing the reaction.

ecosystem. All the living organisms in a community, and the ways in which they react to each other and to their environment.

embryo (adjective **embryonic**). An animal before birth or hatching from egg.

exoskeleton. An invertebrate skeleton which forms the outermost covering of the body, supporting and shaping it.

fertile (verb **fertilise**). Capable of becoming a parent to new individuals.

fry. Newly hatched or young fishes.

habitat. The specific place where a plant or animal lives.

harem. A group of breeding females guarded by a male.

herbivores. Animals which eat plants.

hermaphrodites. Individuals with both female and male reproductive organs. To avoid self-fertilisation, these may not produce eggs and sperm at the same time.

incubate. To keep eggs at a suitable temperature while they develop and hatch.

invertebrate. An animal without a backbone.

larva (plural **larvae**; adjective **larval**). The active immature stage of an animal which undergoes one or more dramatic changes before adulthood.

medusa (plural **medusae**). The free-moving, bell-shaped form of sea jelly, having tentacles around the edge.

moult. To shed exoskeleton to allow increase in size.

notochord. The firm jelly-like rod which supports the body of some advanced invertebrates and embryonic vertebrates.

nutrients. Substances which provide nourishment.

omnivores. Animals which eat both plants and animals.

organisms. Living things.

operculum. A plate-like structure on a gastropod's foot that seals the shell.

parasites (verb **parasitise**; adjective **parasitic**). Animals or plants which live on, or in, other species (the hosts) and take nourishment from them.

pelagic. Of the open ocean or animals living there.

pharynx. The muscular first part of the digestive canal.

pigments. Colouring materials.

polyp. Individual coelenterate animal.

predator. An animal which kills and eats other animals.

primitive. Appearing to be the earliest or very early stage of growth or evolution of an animal.

proboscis. A long, flexible snout.

radial. Arranged like rays going out from a centre.

scavengers. Animals which feed on dead animals they have not killed.

sediment. Matter that settles to the bottom of a liquid, e.g., the silt and organic matter on the sea floor.

sexually. With male and female sex cells involved.

solitary. Living alone.

specialised. Developed in a special way for a special purpose or environment.

species. A group of similar plants or animals which can produce fertile offspring.

sperm (**spermatozoa**). Male reproductive (sex) cells.

spicules. Needle-like or many-branched bodies of lime or silica which support the soft tissues of some marine invertebrates, e.g., sponges.

territory. An area over which an animal establishes control and then defends against other animals of the same species.

toxin (adjective **toxic**). Poison of animal or plant origin.

trilobite. A marine arthropod now extinct but abundant in Cambrian to Permian periods.

uterus. The female organ in which young develop.

venom (adjective **venomous**). Poison produced by an animal such as a scorpionfish, stinging coelenterate, etc.

vertebrate. Describing an animal which has a backbone supporting its spinal cord and a skull protecting its brain.

Map

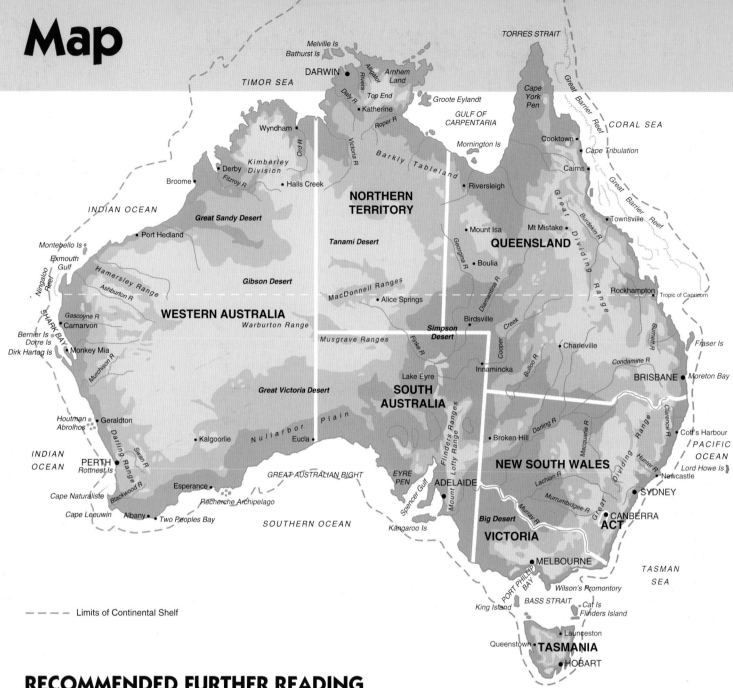

- - - - - Limits of Continental Shelf

RECOMMENDED FURTHER READING

ALLEN, GERALD R. & STEENE, ROGER. 1994. *Indo-Pacific Coral Reef Field Guide*. Tropical Reef Research, Singapore.

BENNETT, ISOBEL. 1992. *Australian Seashores*. Angus & Robertson, Sydney.

COLEMAN, NEVILLE. 1991. *Encyclopedia of Marine Animals*. Angus & Robertson, Sydney.

JONES, D. & MORGAN, G. 1994. *A Field Guide to Crustaceans of Australian Waters*. Reed Books, Sydney.

KNOX, LADIGES & EVANS (eds). 1994. *Biology*. McGraw-Hill Book Company, Sydney.

KUITER, RUDIE H. 1996. *Guide to Sea Fishes of Australia*. New Holland Publishers (Australia), Sydney.

MATHER, PATRICIA & BENNETT, ISOBEL (eds). 1993. *A Coral Reef Handbook*. Surrey Beatty & Sons, Sydney.

PAXTON, J.R. & ESCHMEYER, W.N. 1994. *Encyclopedia of Fishes*. UNSW Press, Sydney.

STRAHAN, RONALD (ed). 1995. *The Mammals of Australia*. Reed Books, Sydney.

READER'S DIGEST. 1984. *The Reader's Digest Book of the Great Barrier Reef*. Sydney.

UNDERWOOD, A.J. & CHAPMAN, M.G. 1995. *Coastal Marine Ecology of Temperate Australia*. UNSW Press, Sydney.

WILSON, B.R. & GILLETT, KEITH. 1971. *Australian Shells*. A.H. & A.W. Reed, Sydney.

PHOTOGRAPHY: Steve Parish (uncredited photographs) and Australia's finest marine photographers: Rob Adland, Kelvin Aitken, Clint Hempsall, Jiri Lochman, Ian Morris, Mark Simmons, Raoul Slater, Geoff Taylor, Neil Wehlack, as credited.

ACKNOWLEDGEMENTS: The author's thanks are due to Dr Lester Cannon for his helpful comments on the text.

First published in Australia by Steve Parish Publishing Pty Ltd
PO Box 1058, Archerfield BC, Queensland 4108 Australia

www.steveparish.com.au

© Copyright Steve Parish Publishing Pty Ltd
ISBN 1-875932-36-4

Series designed by Leanne Nobilio, SPP
Cover designed by Leanne Staff, SPP
Printed in Singapore